And I Only

And I Only

Hattie Annie Jones

BROWN
DOG
BOOKS

Published under licence by Brown Dog Books and
The Self-Publishing Partnership Ltd, 10b Greenway Farm, Bath Rd,
Wick, nr. Bath BS30 5RL

www.selfpublishingpartnership.co.uk

ISBN printed book: 978-1-83952-319-9
ISBN e-book: 978-1-83952-320-5

Cover design by Kevin Rylands
Internal design by Andrew Easton

Printed and bound in the UK

This book is printed on FSC certified paper

For Matthew
1984 to 2016
with love

and for The Helpers

'And I only am escaped alone to tell thee.'

Job 1:15

'O my son Absalom, my son, my son! Would God I had died for thee, O Absalom, my son, my son.'

2 Samuel: 18:33

'The grief we carry is part of the grief of the world. Hold it gently. Let it be honoured. You do not have to keep it in any more. You can let it go into the heart of compassion. You can weep.'

Jack Kornfield: A Meditation on Compassion
www.jackkornfield.com/meditation.grief

Contents

Introduction:

BEWARE AND BE AWARE

This is a weird book, rooted in strangeness. It isn't fiction – but it isn't quite non-fiction, either. It isn't fantasy, despite the elements of fantasy you will find if you read on. It isn't a romance or a history, or a tale of comedy or tragedy – though both comedy and tragedy are present within it. It might be a sort of, kind of memoir – but it isn't a conventional memoir and it lacks a clear chronology. It isn't 'chick lit' or 'misery lit', and it most definitely isn't a tale of triumph over adversity. I talk about adversity, I suppose, but there isn't any triumph. At best it is a story of survival.

When I was sixty-six, and already chronically ill with a neurological disorder, everything I knew about myself, my husband, our marriage, our family and our life was suddenly shattered. This happened some sixteen months after our son, my only child, had ended his own life. The worst that can happen had already happened. And here I meet the inadequacy of words. Alongside my grief for my son, I saw all that I knew of my life disappear over an event horizon and into a black hole. It all disappeared into non-reality, nothingness, along with most of my memories of my husband and our life together. Nothing was as it had seemed. People were transformed from people I'd known into something unrecognisable and dark. I was not who I'd believed myself to be. So who am I?

I belong to a reading group that meets monthly to discuss our chosen books. I remember a fellow member saying to me that she'd enjoyed a particular book we'd read because it had a beginning, a middle and an end, and a clear narrative arc. She probably won't like my book, then, because it has none of these things.

I begin where I begin because I have to begin somewhere, and the moment a few minutes before the Shattering feels to me like the beginning.

I end where I end, in a moment of resolution, because that seems like a good place to end. And I do experience those moments of resolution, of acceptance, but, of course, I don't live there all the time. Grief, for me, is tidal, though it flows in and out less predictably than the ocean. A wave of grief and loss and even despair can overwhelm me at any moment, and I have learned not to struggle. I surrender to the wave when it engulfs me, and trust that it will ultimately carry me back to the shore and back to a feeling of acceptance.

This is a cycle that will end only with my own death, and, since I don't think I'll be doing much communicating after that (though who knows?), I want to communicate what can be communicated of my experience whilst I'm still here to do it.

The middle of my weird book jumps in time and space from here to there and back again in ways that might leave you feeling confused, perhaps unrooted or untethered, unclear about what exactly happened and the sequence of events. It might leave you wondering about the nature of reality and how we know what is real and what isn't. I know this isn't a comfortable feeling – trust me, I really do know – but I hope that you do feel untethered, because that feeling is what I am trying to communicate, to show you. I became untethered. Reality, for me, became unreality, ceased to exist, went out. It became unknowable beyond my own moment-by-moment experience. Memories shimmered and disappeared into the black hole. I lost the threads that connected me to my life. Even now, two years on, I feel myself shimmering in and out of existence. And I had no maps or road signs or beacons or guide ropes to help me navigate my way towards a new reality. I had to make a path through for myself, with many missteps, falls, injuries and wrong turnings along the way. I have had to remind myself to breathe many times, to feel the sensation of my foot on the ground, connecting me to this moment – which is, in fact, all there is to hold on to. I move forward slowly and with caution, step by step, second by second.

And why is any of this of interest to you? Well, maybe it isn't, and so you can return the book to the library or take it to the charity shop. Maybe it's arrogant to think that anyone will be interested in the events and emotions of my life – I've thought about this a lot. But as everyone experiences loss, grief, betrayal and suffering at some point, perhaps there is some value in sharing my experiences and what has helped me to survive?

I offer this weird book because I found strength and encouragement in stories and poems and in the understanding that I am not alone. Everything that happens to me has happened to other people, in life and in fiction, and will happen again in the future. I am part of a web of connectedness. Loss, and grief, and betrayal are common human experiences, and I hope that my weird book might have within it something that could be of use to someone else. I hope it has something to offer, even if you are not facing those issues right at this moment. Writing the weird book has helped guide me through the recent past in relative safety – at least I am not whimpering in the corner, as I might have been. Perhaps that makes it an interesting story despite its weirdness? But you, not I, must be the judge of that.

My colleague in the reading group – the one who likes a clear narrative arc – used to become quite impatient and dismissive when the book we were reading contained elements of fantasy or dreams or flashbacks. She would probably really hate my book, I think, because it contains all of these. Why use imagery to express emotional states when I could just say 'I feel sad' or angry or whatever? But I prefer to try to show you the feeling, rather than tell you about it. Telling rather than showing can create a distance from the feeling rather than giving you the immediacy of it. The untethered space traveller floating to his death evokes, for me at least, my feelings in the aftermath of the Shattering far more powerfully than any description. I was lost in the deepest darkness and being drawn further and further from safety and from everything I knew. I thought I might be dying. Perhaps I hoped I might be dying?

Although my book lacks a clear chronology and leaves unanswered questions, although it is told largely through metaphor rather than being straightforwardly factual, although the imagery may seem strange at times, and although the book may leave you feeling a little lost and untethered, I hope that as you read on, it will make its own kind of sense for you.

I am not going to explain everything – there is much I don't know and life does not always make sense. There are parts of the book where I want you to find your own meaning, though I will explain a little as we go along about what the various images have meant to me.

If we travel together for a few miles, then I am grateful for your company. If, like the woman from my reading group, you prefer to take a different path, then take it with my best wishes for your journey. May you find your own dragons in your own way and in your own time. They will be there when you need them.

Love,
Hattie x

− 1 −

MY LIFE IS
AS I KNOW IT TO BE.

My life is as I know it to be. It has a familiar, if imperfect, pattern, just like everyone else's life. I am an atom in a stream of light, moving from somewhere to somewhere else, because there has to be a beginning and there has to be an ending. 'Handwriting is closest to the heart', or words to that effect. You are reading this in print, but I am writing it in pen, in a notebook, quaintly old-fashioned. Does writing this by hand make my words more truthful? The distancing created by the keyboard and computer screen − does that create more layers between the truth of a moment of experience and the description of that moment? The description can only be a construct, something undertaken once the moment itself has passed − the moment as recalled, not the moment as experienced.

The Moment as Recalled: I am in a narrow, dimly lit hospital corridor. C, my stepson, is close by. Over to my left is the seemingly peaceful world of the High Dependency Unit where my husband lies, partly here, partly somewhere else, monitored by machines and observed by careful nurses. He may be asleep. He is quiet, motionless, possibly unaware.

There is a disturbance, a shimmering, in the air around me, left by the young HDU doctor, Oliver. I met him this morning, noticed his dark good looks, his kind face, his willingness to explain events as they happen around us. Hours later, he is still here, coming to speak to us, to warn us, to prepare us as gently but honestly as he can for what might happen. He has just left. I wonder if he can go home at last?

Now, early October, it is dark outside. It might be raining – I have an image of light, glistening and glittering in puddles in the darkness. Windows. In memory I am close to windows.

How far can I rely on the complexity of memory? Some of this must be false. The physical geography of the hospital is not as I remember it, but maybe the memory represents a kind of truth, a felt truth, rather than a literal fact.

There is a feeling of timelessness, isolation, separateness from past, present and the imagined future. I am a space traveller, floating in emptiness, tethered – how securely? – by a slender lifeline to the spaceship and survival. I know, in this moment, the shape of my imperfect life.

The moment passes – more significant in memory than at the time. I did not know that it was the final moment of my familiar life, one of those 'before and after' moments when everything changes, becomes strange.

There is a shattering. Not a glass bowl crashing to pieces on my tiled floor. Something else – a far-off warning rumbling, creaking, and then a hairline crack appearing in the ice, spreading, radiating outwards, creating fissures, moving from a rumbling to staccato gunfire and, finally, the roar of a structure collapsing in ruins, the ice shelf falling away.

Now, months on from that recalled moment, I feel like an archaeologist. I collect up the fragments that might once have composed my life. I turn them over and around, examine them closely, peer through my specs to see how they fit together. Some of the pieces match closely, fit together easily, make up a pattern that is recognisable. Others, though, have suffered more damage, have lost part of their substance to the crushing weight of earth and time. I can see that these fragments might once have formed a pot, whose ghost I hold in my hands, but they no longer quite fit together. There can be a kind of pot, reconstructed from these pieces, but there are holes and gaps and a part of the pattern has been destroyed. There is something to see here – an artefact for a museum – but there is no whole or usable pot.

I try to recapture **The Moment as Experienced**, but that moment passed in a moment. I can only give a narrative, as close to the factual reality of the moment as memory allows – but with what overlays, distortions and simple errors created by time and emotion? I am baffled by the impossibility of truth. Whose truth is true?

Oliver, C and I all had our roles in this moment. We all experienced it together, but in our own individual ways, and we each have our own truth. For Oliver, it is a moment in a long day of moments, some spent delivering bad news. He may not even remember me or our moment at all. Yet we are connected, Oliver and I, and I will never forget him.

He is young, Oliver, young enough to be my son. My son. But I have no son – no daughter, either – nobody carries my genetic narrative into the future. This is, perhaps, a good thing. I end with me. He is also kind, Oliver, with a gentle manner and a concerned face. He makes very reasonable assumptions about my long marriage. I make them too. This is almost the very last moment in which these assumptions can hold any truth. We have a distant, but friendly, marriage. We have a shared history, shared humour, shared sadness, shared concern for each other, for the wider family, for the world. We are caring people, trying to lead honest lives. There is a pattern. Not the pattern I might have chosen, but I make the best of it, believing my husband to be doing the same. Joint effort. Joint endeavour.

I am, of course, on the other side of that life, that reality, now. Time has passed, as time does. I can barely remember what that pattern felt like in the living of it, because it was shattered so comprehensively, utterly destroyed.

But is it possible to destroy something that never existed?

Maybe that pattern wasn't shattered or swallowed into non-existence by a black hole. Nothing so profound or dramatic. Maybe it just went 'pop' and disappeared, never having been there in the first place. Not like a soap bubble. Even a soap bubble can leave traces, a smear, a tiny rainbow. A soap bubble exists, if only for a second. Maybe the pattern of my life was a thirty-year illusion, smoke and mirrors, created by the kind of magician who works with misdirection. 'Real', Merlin-like magicians, if they exist, manipulate the material world. They have power over the physical world that they can use for good or ill. Magicians using misdirection – illusionists – manipulate nothing except our perceptions of the world, our brain. 'Look over here!' shouts Misdirection. 'Don't look over there...' No, that's wrong. Misdirection doesn't shout. Misdirection whispers, offers subliminal suggestion, makes us think we are choosing of our own free will to look over here, not over there, when, in fact, Misdirection limits and controls our choices.

The word 'gaslighting' comes into my mind, a usage I only came across recently. The reference is to the play and film *Gaslight*. If you don't know it, you can look it up. A woman being made to doubt herself, her perceptions, her reality as experienced being made unreal through misdirection, manipulation, deceit.

I keep circling around this moment of the Shattering, but I'm never quite touching it, am I? Let's make contact. My husband and our thirty-four-year marriage were constructs, illusions, with no reality. My image of myself as an intelligent and perceptive woman popped out of existence too. Not so intelligent, not so perceptive. A cliché. A stereotype. Worse than a cliché – a victim? Though I reject that label. A wronged (and wrong) woman, betrayed and deceived over half a lifetime, married to Deacon Brodie or Mr Hyde. 'I have a dark side,' said my husband, days after the moment of change had passed. He did indeed.

I am still procrastinating, aren't I? You may have noticed, if you are counting, that I have written 2,641 words without saying what actually happened in this moment when everything changed. I move towards it, then glance off it, move away. It was a real moment. It happened, one way or another: either as I describe it or some other way.

Have you forgotten Oliver? His role was to describe what the doctors knew so far of my husband's condition. Just to set the scene – my husband had been admitted, close to death, to the High Dependency Unit of our local hospital. For months, he refused to talk honestly to doctors, despite my concern and the concern of others. I had 'kidnapped' him when he became too weak to resist, and taken him to get medical help. Had I not done this on Friday, said Oliver, my husband would certainly not have survived the weekend. During the eighteen months since our son's death, I had woken daily with the thought that this might be the day I would find my husband dead – and this, according to Oliver, was a realistic fear. Now, thirty-six hours later – another cliché. There was good news and bad news. He was alive and they were able to treat him, and had other treatment options (well, one other treatment option) in reserve. However, he had done himself so much damage through avoidance and delay that realistically speaking, he may not survive the weekend anyway. We should be hopeful – I had given him a chance – but we should be prepared that he might die in the next few hours.

Oliver now leaves the stage and my stepson's role in this moment comes to the fore. There are people we should speak to, warn, prepare. We can, he says, get contact details for these people from my husband's phone, which my husband had handed to me so I could get the phone number for one of his counselling supervisees and cancel their next supervision.

This phone – a Blackberry, such a benign name for something that had such a toxic impact – this phone is not easy to navigate. C, more accustomed than I am to smartphones, is trying to get into my husband's list of contacts, but he is failing, defeated by the tiny keyboard, the roller ball, the confusion of icons. Frustrated, he hands the phone to me, open not at the address book, but at a list of text messages.

I see a message from Peter. Brilliant! This is the person I need to contact to cancel the supervision meeting. Next is a message from another Peter, Peter C, my husband's half-brother and someone else we need to contact. I'm on a roll now. For once, something is going right. The next message is from Linda, my husband's half-sister. They met twenty-four years ago, when he traced his birth family. He was adopted, and his adoption had cast long shadows over his life, and I'd hoped for some healing when we traced his birth family.

Time slows down now. Linda is important. I'm glad we've found her number. I open the message, intending to scroll down to her number, which will be at the end of the message thread.

14/06/14 @ 22.34:
I wish you weren't working and you were here. I want to snuggle up in bed and make love. Missing my lollipop (smiley face). Want a cuddle and to kiss you all over. Love and kisses. Linda xxxxxx

And already I am distorting reality. There were two similar text messages, as I discovered much later, after my husband's death. Was this the one I saw? I'm no longer sure. The other one has been deleted somewhere along the line by somebody – maybe even me, I don't know. It doesn't matter. You get the gist.

Time stops. I freeze. C can't see this. 'Stupid phone,' I say,' I can't get my head round it. I'll try later.' Phone off. Out of sight, in my bag. Make normal conversation with C. You will contact that person, I will contact this one.

I hear that rumbling, louder now, the warning, moving closer. I move and speak automatically, talk to C, say goodnight to hospital staff. 'Ring us any time, day or night, if you are worried,' they say. 'Thank you.'

I notice a feeling of surprise that no one seems to notice that I am now an automaton, moving stiffly, jerkily, speaking in mindless, scripted fashion. I am a wife bot.

The biggest part of my mind is reverberating, shivering in shock. My husband has been fucking his sister – perhaps not very recently, he is incapable now, but 2014? Three and a half years ago? My mind races round the library of what I know about adoption, genetic sexual attraction, incest, infidelity, betrayal, lies, more lies, genetic sexual attraction, the power of it… But the central shocking fact. My husband has been fucking his sister. His sister has been fucking my husband.

Look in on my husband – still sleeping or away somewhere else. Still potentially dying. Say goodbye to C quickly – we need to go home. Walk back in the darkness and the rain to my car. Drive home, very, very carefully. Lights reflecting on the wet road – was it really raining? Or is it that I felt it should be raining?

Responsibility. Lock the car. Pay attention to the dogs. Give them clean water. Walk them round the block.

My Husband Has Been Fucking Linda, His Sister. My husband – the clergyman, therapist, all-round caring person – has been fucking his sister.

I sit in the kitchen and shake. I should turn on the light. I should eat. Do I have a drink? I don't remember. Whisky? I hope I had some in the cupboard.

Surprisingly, I sleep. And sleep. I don't remember whether I dreamed. I hope not.

Sunday: 5.30 a.m. I wake up. My first thought – 'Linda wouldn't do that.' My husband has not been fucking his sister. There is another Linda, the Linda whose message thread starts with her lollipop and ends with her response to whatever message my husband sent her in the week in May, 2016, when our son, my only child, took his own life. 'Awww,' she says, 'big hugs xxxx'. Strangely, my son's death feels bigger than 'Awww, big hugs xxxx'. This is not my husband's sister.

That was Sunday morning, 8 October 2017. The rumbling had intensified, the cracks were beginning to cover all the surface. Reflecting now, eight months later, on that day, it seems strange that my thought was, *Linda wouldn't do that*. What does it mean that I don't remember thinking, *My husband wouldn't do that*? What did I know, on some unconscious level, without knowing that I knew it?

I know I heard the rumbling, saw the cracks spreading,

slowly at first and then with increasing speed. My life as I knew it disappeared. What now? What next? I feel sick. I am sick. I think, *Thank god I have a tiled floor.* It makes it easier to clean up the vomit that was my life.

Who is this Other Linda, the Un-sister, the Lady of the Lollipops and Big Hugs? Don't forget the xxxxxx. 'Who is it that can tell me who I am?' Or who anyone else might be?

– 2 –

HIC SUNT DRACONES
'HERE BE DRAGONS'

This is the story of my life, but my life intersects with the lives of others, and their stories are their own. I can say what I saw or surmised of the experience of others, but that will be my perception of their experience, not the experience itself. I am not, in this story, an omniscient narrator – sadly, because if I were, it would be a very different narrative.

It is a story of shapeshifting, of blurred identities, alternate realities and confusion. The person masquerading under my husband's sister's phone number was, in fact, the Un-Linda, the Lollipop Lady – though without the high-vis jacket and 'Stop!' sign. In fact, without any clothes at all.

As I think about my marriage, I am 'buffering' – have I said that before? I may have done, because it is my day-to-day reality, even now, many months on from the Shattering. I lived for thirty-four years in a marriage in which I knew, or thought

I knew, or believed I knew, the shape, feel, texture and quality of our shared lives. Had a cartographer drawn a map of my marriage – my life – he (or she) would have needed to write on that map the words used by early map-makers when they reached the limit of the known world or an area they knew to be perilous – 'Here Be Dragons'. (And I remember that we always rather liked dragons, my son and I. A favourite film of his childhood was *Flight of Dragons*, and I loved it too. But dragons are ambiguous, aren't they? Unknown and unexplored territory may be dangerous…)

I turn to *Wikipedia*, reliable enough for this, and find the following:

'*Here Be Dragons* means dangerous or unexplored territories, in imitation of a medieval practice of putting illustrations of dragons, sea monsters and other mythological creatures on uncharted areas of maps.'

Scrolling down, I find:

'*Here Be Dragons* is a very interesting sentence!' said Thomas Sander, editor of the *Portolan*, the journal of the Washington Map Society. 'In early maps you would see images of sea monsters; it was a way to say there's bad stuff out there.'

There is indeed bad stuff out there in the unchartered hinterland in which I find myself on – let's be specific – Sunday 8 October 2017. I'd fallen down a wormhole in space, emerging in a world of weirdness and shifting identities. Other people looked the same. My house, my car, my dogs all looked the same as they had twenty-four hours earlier. There was a kind of 'uncanny valley effect' at work, though – everything looked the same, but not quite. Something was 'off'. Everybody and everything was different. Reality had changed – so it can't have been reality. My life as I had known it to be was not my life. Pop! It vanished.

I am trapped – am I screaming? Beating the air with my fists? – in the interface between knowledge and belief. I write, *My life as I had known it to be*. But I had not **known** – I had only believed that I knew. So we move into a kind of multiverse, an alternative reality. *My life as I had known it to be* was illusory, un-knowledge; ignorance, in fact. Delusion, even.

'Here Be Dragons.' But where are the dragonslayers when you really need them? I am alone. Do you recall my original image of the collapsing ice shelf? I am in the ice-cold waters at the edge of the world. No one survives here for long. I am lost in the frozen vastness of outer space. No umbilical cord. If I can manage to reach earth, land, the dragons are waiting, circling, hungry.

There are no dragonslayers, no rescuers.

I am alone.

– 3 –

THE KEY TO CONTROL

Something I remember from my counselling training – 'the key to control is knowing that control is neither possible nor necessary'. I don't remember who said it – somebody did – but it has stayed with me.

It's hard to think that life is random. We look for patterns. We tell ourselves that we are managing the direction our lives are taking, that we are in control – but then Life has an unpleasant habit of slamming us into a wall, just to show us how wrong we are, and maybe, to teach us humility. Hubris leads inevitably to nemesis.

Q: What makes God laugh?

A: Watching us make plans.

Life is random. We might as well accept that 'resistance is futile' and allow ourselves to be assimilated. I might have a T-shirt printed – I DON'T FLOG DEAD HORSES. Or another one – CHOOSE YOUR BATTLES WISELY. Or – my favourite – SHIT HAPPENS.

My son would have recognised the Star Trek reference in the previous paragraph. He and I had some shared tastes and interests that seemed to leave my husband a bit bemused. Our discussions around whether we preferred David Tennant or Matt Smith as Dr Who left him cold. He complained that we were cleverer than him – this seems a little ironic now. Nonetheless, maybe that perception, true or not, was a real grievance for him, something that allowed him to justify to himself the fact that he could *get one over on us*, fool us – well, me. I'm not sure my son was completely fooled. After all, once the truth was out there, my husband said – several times – that one of Lovely Linda's attractions for him was that she presented him with no intellectual challenge; or did he say *threat*? I can't remember.

For my son and I, Marvin the Paranoid Android expressed a profound truth. 'Life? Don't talk to me about life.' Spoken in a suitably lugubrious tone of voice. We knew, my son and I, how little control we really had. 'Resistance is futile. You will be assimilated.' We knew the meaning of life – it is six times seven, or forty-two. We knew quite a lot about dragons too. I remember that somebody else said that life must be lived forwards, but can only be understood backwards. That's no help now, really.

But sometimes we looked like a family, the three of us. Sometimes we even felt like a family. We argued, agreed, disagreed, laughed at shared jokes and expressed shared sadnesses. We debated politics or why we did/didn't like football. We ate curries, compared notes on real ales and the relative merits of single malt whiskies (me) or different kinds of vodka (my husband). We watched *Have I Got News For You* on TV together and talked about Thomas Hobbes. We explored shared memories. There was a superficial resemblance to a family, but it felt more real than that at the time, to me, at least. My son's reality was his own. My husband seems to have lived in many realities, each isolated in its own strongbox.

One of my husband's favourite jokes:

A baby polar bear goes to his dad and says, 'Daddy, am I a real polar bear?' 'Of course you are,' says his dad. 'Your mum's a polar bear, I'm a polar bear, your grandma and grandad are real polar bears... so you are a real polar bear too.'

The baby polar bear was troubled, though, so went to ask his big brother. 'Big Brother, am I a real polar bear?' 'Of course you are,' says his big brother. 'Mum and Dad are polar bears, I'm a polar bear, Grannie and Grandad are polar bears... so you are a real polar bear too.'

The baby polar bear worked his way through the entire family, always asking the same question and always getting the same reply. Finally, he went to his mother and said, 'Mummy, am I a real polar bear?'

His mother said, 'Of course you are a real polar bear, darling. But why do you keep asking? What is worrying you?'

'Well, Mummy,' the baby replied, 'if I'm a real polar bear, why am I so fucking cold?'

Should I have been asking, 'Are we a REAL family?' But I did ask, and received very believable answers about how my husband felt that his difficult childhood had made close relationships hard for him, and about how clergy families often have issues because the emotional demands of the job can leave relatively little emotional energy for marriage and family life – etc., etc. He cared about me, he assured me, and was doing his best. I believed him. Did I, though? Did I REALLY believe him? Or did I simply choose to believe him? Disallow doubt?

What remains now of the family we did or didn't have is grief – grief for my son's life and death.

My son, who loved Terry Pratchett's novels, decided to take the advice of DEATH in *Good Omens*. 'DON'T THINK OF IT AS DYING… JUST THINK OF IT AS LEAVING EARLY TO AVOID THE RUSH.'

He left early, at thirty-one, my son, my only child. He avoided the rush. There is no one else in the world with whom I can have those 7 a.m. conversations about six times seven and the meaning of life. Resistance is futile. I am alone. Grief fills up the space that my son used to occupy. The dragons are still circling, still watching, still waiting…

Shakespeare, whose son Hamnet died aged eleven – he knew about grief. He gave the following words to a mother (to fit the shape of the play. Fathers grieve too):

'*Grief fills the room up of my absent child, Lies in his bed, walks up and down with me…*'

Grief sits in my son's place on the ottoman in my conservatory. Grief guides my hand to the smaller cafetière now, for my early morning coffee-making ritual. Grief takes me for a pizza at the Café Roma, or, perhaps, for a curry somewhere else. Grief comes with me to the supermarket and reminds me to put the no-longer-needed crunchy peanut butter back on the shelf. Grief bids me goodnight as I fall asleep and then sits by my bed, waiting patiently for me to wake up.

I walk, talk, move, do things, even enjoy things, but even whilst I laugh or smile, Grief is my ever-present companion.

I am alone. I am never alone. Grief never deserts me, neglects me or abandons me, but stays with me always. We are conjoined, Grief and I, floating together in the darkness and the cold, aware of the dragons and mythical monsters out of sight, but all around us, ever watchful.

Beside this greater grief, all other griefs diminish. Do I grieve for my husband? That's a bigger question than it seems. I did not know my husband. How do I grieve for a stranger, a man I never met? 'Any man's death diminishes me,' said John Donne in 1624. Death, for the person who dies, is, as far as we can know, the end of that person's life. Each death, though, is an event in the lives of the survivors. There are repercussions, shock waves, earthquakes, even, for those who remain. There is more to be said about how I grieve for my husband, and who it is that I grieve for – but not now.

For now I take my place in the line of grieving mothers that stretches back to the beginning of consciousness and maybe even beyond. We know grief at a cellular level. The body vibrates with grief as we stand in this line that nobody wants to join.

Sometimes I walk my dogs round a lake. My husband used to come with us most days, my son sometimes. Now it is just the four of us – me, the two dogs and Grief.

We watch the swans, with their seeming serenity, sailing over the lake. My dogs are terriers – they will chase anything – but they watch the swans with a wary respect.

We have walked here several times a week, sometimes twice a day, for the last six years – and before that, for the ten years from 1987, when my son was two, to 1997, when we moved to the vicarage. Had you remembered that my husband was, among other things, a clergyman? We lived in a vicarage for sixteen years, our little family – and don't forget the Lovely Lady of the Lollipops, who visited for some of those years when my son and I were out of the way. She left no trace in the air of my home, no imprint on the cushions. Apparently, she walked my dogs. The dogs kept the secret.

Every spring for the last six years, a pair of swans has nested in the same place, almost hidden in the undergrowth on the lakeside where we walk. Is it the same pair? I think so. Swans can live for twenty or thirty years, after all. Swans, unlike people, mate for life – and tend to remain faithful to one partner to maximise their chances of rearing the maximum number of young. Ducks are less monogamous, it seems, but swans find fidelity a good strategy.

Every year I look forward to seeing the swans hatch their cygnets, and then watching the cygnets grow to maturity. I think of one of this pair of swans as Big Daddy Swan (though why do I assume this is the male bird?). He – let's stick with my belief that this is Daddy Swan – is slightly larger and surely more aggressive than all the other swans. He plants himself by the path and hisses from a distance at passing dog walkers and dogs. I've always assumed he is protecting his family. That's how it seems.

This year there were six eggs in the nest. Then the shrubs

sprouted bigger leaves, more flowers, and I could no longer see the nest.

One sunny morning, there were six cygnets swimming on the lake. Lovely. A full house of hatchlings.

A few days later, only four, then three a couple of days after that. Finally there was just one. Never mind. Let's watch this last, solitary ugly duckling turn into a swan.

Yesterday the dogs and I walked round the lake. No cygnet. We walked round again, just in case we'd missed him the first time. Still no cygnet. We talked to the other dog walkers (I think of us all as the Confederation of Dog Walkers. We talk to each other and know the names, not of each other but of each other's dogs.) Yesterday was Monday. The cygnet has not been seen since Saturday.

Swans glide to the edge of the lake, expecting food. I have no way to know which of these swans built the nest over there. Big Daddy Swan has gone from the path.

Does the mother swan grieve for her six lost cygnets?

I do.

The life of my own lost child had ended some seventeen months before that moment in the hospital corridor that I have called 'the Shattering'. I needed his presence then, but all that was present was his absence. Like the cygnet, he was gone, his possessions divided amongst his friends or finding a home in my house, his body reduced to ash. Should I tell you more about him? I'm not sure, any more than I'm sure where or how his story fits into this weird book. But we gave him life, my husband and I, and he is part of this story.

– 4 –

'THERE'S NO SMOKE…'

'… **without fire.**' Everybody knows that, don't they? I'm sure I've probably said it myself at some time in the past, and I bet you have too. 'There's no smoke without fire.' Such an obvious, commonsensical statement, isn't it – the sort of thing we instinctively know to be true. 'No smoke without fire,' we say wisely, our heads nodding in collective wisdom as we condemn somebody on the basis of gossip, rumour and speculation. An allegation has been made or implied, after all, and we may feel that it is both credible and true. We don't need actual evidence to assume guilt because we all know that there is no smoke without fire. Do you think it's possible, though, that this piece of conventional wisdom is more conventional than wise? More about lazy thinking than about understanding or truth? Ask the many women burned as witches in the sixteenth and seventeenth centuries. Ask Leon Brittan or Cliff Richard. Ask my son.

I begin – And yet… But where do I even start to unpack what is wrong and cruel and vicious about this gobbet of popular wisdom? Is it possible that the air can be full of foul, thick, choking smoke where there is no fire at all? Fire or not, this smoke can still kill you. It helped kill my son.

Is it possible, too, that a hard, aggressive fire can burn without there being much smoke at all? Like the fires eating their way underground through moorland peat? Such fires can cause immense damage and destruction with very little visible sign, little if any smoke, unless you stand in exactly the right place and look very closely. Rather like my husband, in fact. A few months after the Shattering, I watched the moors near my home burning savagely, huge plumes of black smoke visible for miles. After many days, the fires seemed under control, the smoke disappeared – and yet below the earth the fire continued to burn, moving through the peat, travelling underground and out of sight, ready to attack again.

There's another piece of popular wisdom – 'a picture is worth a thousand words'. Well, I can't draw.

Me And My Smaller Dog.

See? I told you I can't draw. But maybe, even though I can't draw, I can use words to illustrate what happened, to give you the image and the feeling of all that took place. Words can explain why I can only spit out, 'There's no smoke without fire,' and why, if I hear you say it, I want to punch you in the face. But don't worry. I might want to punch you, but I won't. I have my fists under control. I think. Let me draw you a picture…

Once upon a time, in some part of the multiverse, there was a young man named Murf. He had been a baby and a child, of course, before he was a young man. Born too soon and too ill, expelled into a cold December from his mother's inhospitable womb, baby Murf was close to death. The cleverest wizards worked long, hard hours, using their finest magic, to save Murf's life, and they eventually succeeded. There was rejoicing in the land.

Murf grew into a clever, engaging child, described as 'frighteningly bright' by the wizards employed to teach him. He loved stories and animals and exploring new places, new foods, new sensations. He was curious about everything. He had a strong sense of fairness and was alive to the suffering of others. All was not well with Murf, though, and he sometimes seemed like someone who lacked a layer of skin, unfitted for the cruelties of the world.

Life was not always kind to him. As well as being born before his time and dangerously ill, he was born with *talipes* (club-footedness) and as soon as the intensive-care wizards had finished with him, he needed daily physio to help his feet develop normally. He had some early problems with communication – there were certain sounds he struggled to make, and this made his speech unintelligible to most people. The speech-therapy wizards were summoned, and by the time Murf was five and a half, he could speak fluently. Nothing in life came easily for Murf – asthma led to breathing problems, *talipes* led to delayed walking and discomfort, his phonological disorder led to speech problems and difficulties in making relationships with his peers, and his intelligence isolated him sometimes. And it can be dangerous in this life to be different or unusual...

As he grew into adolescence and young manhood, he became, like most of us, a mixture of virtues and failings, strengths and vulnerabilities. Strengths and vulnerabilities sound like opposites, don't they? But maybe it's possible that sometimes a personal quality that seems like, and is, a strength can also be something that makes you vulnerable. And so it was with Murf, sadly.

One of his strengths was that he could empathise with people, particularly those people who are marginalised or disadvantaged. He found life difficult himself sometimes, so understood from the inside what it feels like to struggle with life's darkness. This ability to empathise is surely a strength?

I've already mentioned that Murf could seem like someone with a layer of skin missing, with insufficient protection against life, the world and other people, and this became more apparent, and more difficult, as Murf grew up. The pain of human existence weighed heavily upon him, feeding and growing the pain he carried within his own psyche. (He probably would have rejected the word *soul*.) I've already given away the ending, and you already know that they didn't all live happily ever after. I can't ask Murf whether he'd prefer *psyche* or *soul* because he is dead, having taken his own life at the age of thirty-one years, four months and twenty-six days. He died alone. All that he had been became a pile of fine, grey ash, gritty on my fingers. He had stayed as long as he could, I think.

Murf's final two or three years were harsh and barren. I write this – my hands write the words – but their meaning drives hooks through my flesh and I bleed. I look at the page and feel surprise that all I can see are the words. The page should be soaked in blood. My mind glances off the hard surfaces of reality, refuses to look, has to be made to look, to see. I must look, must see, must set down Murf's story as best I can. It is not his story, of course, because he is not here to tell his story. I can only tell it as it seemed to me.

I am sitting at my kitchen table to write this. It's Sunday afternoon. We are on the cusp of a new year. I hear Murf coming in through the back door, my dogs jumping up in welcome. I can see him framed in the kitchen doorway, his long leather coat flapping around his legs as he moves. He seems about to say something…

And then my dog barks again. I look away, look back, and of course Murf is gone. Not gone, because he wasn't there to begin with. Just empty air where he stood three years ago, and the dog barking to tell me to get up and take him for a walk.

You will not have forgotten, alert reader that you are, that Murf was my son. I am – was? Am? – what tense should I use? I am his mother. But there is no longer any Murf, so I am nobody's mother. Some of Murf's cremains – that fine grey ash I mentioned earlier – went up into the sky, fired in rockets by his friends at his 'Going Away Party and Final Aerial Transit'. The rest of that fine grey ash rests in a felt casket, melting into the earth in the churchyard of the church where Murf's father presided as priest every Sunday. I tucked Murf's ashes into that casket as I'd tucked him into his bed thirty years earlier, wanting him to be warm and safe.

This is my son, my baby, my boy – no longer alive in the world. I did not, could not, save him, just as he could not save himself. I failed. And as I failed him in the days leading up to his death, so I failed him throughout his life by failing to see the deceit at the heart of our family, polluting and poisoning the air we breathed. I failed to protect myself, and in failing to protect myself, I failed to protect my child.

FAIL. The word has a heavy sound, like the tolling of a funeral bell.

FAIL. Its heaviness follows me through each day, sometimes close and other times fainter and more distant.

FAIL. It never goes away. I hear it now.

I also hear the words of consolation offered to me by caring, well-meaning people. 'You did your best.' 'He was an adult – it was his choice.' 'He knew he was loved.' All true. I tell myself these words and listen to them when they are spoken by others.

I did my best. I did. I really did. But I know in every cell of my body that in the last few weeks of Murf's life, my best, exhausted as I felt, was not very good. **FAIL.**

But I've digressed, haven't I? I began to tell you Murf's story, and then diverged from the beginning to tell you about his ending. You will find that I do this diverging, meandering, quite a lot. One thought leads to another and another and I find myself not exactly where I'd planned to be, but somewhere else. I trust that my own soul, my own psyche, leads me off into these wanderings for a reason. There is some purpose to it, even though I may not always know what it is. I trust my unconscious mind to know what it is doing.

You may be asking yourself why I tell my stories in this allusive, metaphorical way, using images rather than straightforward descriptions of fact. Facts are slippery things, though, aren't they? – just as words can be slippery, their meaning sliding around and elusive. Am I being evasive? – Avoiding painful truths? Am I protecting myself? Protecting Murf, who might not have wanted me to tell his story? Protecting other people? I believe I am trying to be honest, but I can't know for sure, can I? What is out of my awareness is out of my awareness, after all. There are 'unknown unknowns'.

Is it possible that the images and metaphors I use come as close as is possible to what is hidden behind and away from my conscious self? That they build a bridge between my conscious mind and the deeper, more hidden understanding that lies in my unconscious mind? I remember a dream I had years ago, at time when, unknown to me, much was happening behind my back and my home was being used as a place of assignation by my husband and his Lollipop Lady. In the dream I was walking my Border Terrier (in truth, my favourite dog – but don't tell anyone). We were walking around a circular path where I used to go quite often. In the centre of the circle is a large grassy area, with trees and benches where weary dog walkers can sit. Along one arc of the path is some dense shrubbery – overgrown rhododendrons and other bushes. As we walked past this shrubbery, as vivid in the dream as in life, a huge crocodile suddenly lunged out of the bushes and seized my little dog in its jaws, disappearing as silently as it had come. I was left holding just the snapped-off end of the dog lead in my hand. And then I woke up, sweating, heart racing, and went downstairs to check that my dog was safe.

What was that dream trying to tell me about threat and destructiveness? About wrongness, something out of its place – there are not too many crocodiles roaming in parks in the north of England. The truths told in poetry, in imagery, in dreams may be closest to the heart, to the bone.

I feel I am trying to find a way into the emotional truth of our lives, the truth behind the facts. I say this tentatively, always aware that things are often not what they seem and that self-deception can be as perilous as deception by others. How do I trust my perceptions or my judgement, knowing how these have failed me? The past is a place of shapeshifting, sandstorm-blighted, fog-bound confusion. The future is unknown. I am here, now, and this is how I live these stories in this moment.

All I can tell you is this. After Murf made his decision and ended his life, I found myself in an alternate universe, a different world. I clung to the thought that somewhere in the multiverse, versions of us lived in a different reality, where

Murf flourished. Later, when my husband became more ill, and deceptions were exposed, all my worlds shattered and scattered into fragments and my memories of my marriage disappeared into non-existence. Where am I? Who am I? Who can I be when nothing is real, not even myself? I can – and have – related the event of those few years in a straightforward narrative arc in the business-like settings of my life. This is what happened. This is what this person said and did, what I said and did. I have had to do that for various reasons at various times. And to tell these stories in that way is easier, less painful, less revealing of myself than telling it as I am telling it to you. I keep my clothes on when I tell these stories in that factual and chronological way. When I tell them through the images and sensations and dreams and nightmares of my life, I feel naked in front of you. This is what it felt like, and this is more real, has greater emotional truth, than any more straightforward telling could have.

Because in the end, I am not really telling you Murf's story, or my husband's story, am I? I am telling you my story, and how I imagine their realities to have been. And I want to be as honest as I can be. Images and metaphors contain truths. In calling Murf 'Sir Murf', something of his character appears. As a boy, he loved playing Warhammer, and because we lived in an area of inadequate public transport, I used to ferry him to and from his games. I still have a box of the figures he painted. We used to talk in the car, often about the game he'd played and often about the Bretonnian Knights – he liked them. He liked their sense of honour and fairness, their focus on integrity despite their limitations, and we agreed that he might be a bit of a Bretonnian himself. 'Sir' Murf.

Sir Murf of the Dragon's Cave

Smoke. Fire. We will get back to the smoke and the fire eventually, and I will tell you what I can know of Murf's story. I am telling you these stories of our lives – mine, my husband's and Murf's – in the only way I can tell them, untethered as I am. You are free to read them, or to put the book down. Your choice.

- 5 -

AM I A REAL POLAR BEAR?

I think that perhaps I am getting the hang of this multiverse thing now. There is the me who is floating and freezing in an icy sea. There is the me in my spacesuit, marooned in the even colder vacuum of deep space. I can no longer see the spaceship. I can move at will now from one of these realities to the other. I have some choices, it seems. I haven't forgotten the dragons, but they can only get me if I end up back on land. They are not an immediate danger – and I'm making assumptions here, aren't I? Are they a danger at all?

My son used to mock my pretensions to any kind of scientific understanding, and I'm fairly sure he was right to do so. However, this is my version of the multiverse, and my son is not here to tell me that I'm wrong.

I remember, as a teenager, watching a film on TV about the sinking of the *Titanic*. It was quite an old film even then, fifty odd years ago – it was called *A Night To Remember*, and I think it was made in 1958, when I would have been seven.

We will return to the *Titanic* later. My husband and the *Titanic* are inextricably linked in my mind. He seems to have regarded himself as *unsinkable*, and failed, inexcusably, to foresee the circumstances that would prove him wrong. Like the *Titanic*, he did not carry enough lifeboats for everyone on board. Like the captain of the *Titanic*, he went down with his ship.

For now, though, I remember from that film and maybe from later reading, that the cries of the people in the water continued for quite a long time – maybe even an hour. I have read that you can survive for a while in freezing water, and that most deaths are caused by drowning rather than hypothermia. The initial, very brief, cold shock response to immersion can make you gasp and, if your head goes underwater, lead to drowning. Of course, you may panic, which reduces your chances further. The shock may also trigger a heart attack, especially in people with already damaged hearts. I suppose that might be me. If you manage to survive those first dangers, your ability to help yourself will decline after about ten minutes, as your body focuses on maintaining core body heat and cuts off the blood flow to your extremities.

Your chances of survival are better if you are wearing a flotation device, which will help save you from drowning, if you are able to avoid shivering (how?) and if help is close by or you are able, somehow, to get yourself out of the water. You do not have long. Hypothermia will get you – if you survive the other dangers of cold-water immersion – after about thirty to sixty minutes. I don't know if I can avoid shivering. I have no flotation device. I won't survive for long here in this cold, cold water – but there is some small chance of survival.

For my other self, floating in space, with only the oxygen in my spacesuit to breathe, death looks certain. Nobody can help me and there seems to be nothing I can do to help myself. I float, weightless and powerless, my umbilical cord useless, connected to nothing. I'm adrift and far away from the spaceship now. I don't think that the Tardis is coming. I am on my own.

I still have a choice, though, I realise. I can continue to float and wait for my oxygen to run out – this will not take long. Then I will die. Or I can take control of the situation – in a strange way – and loosen or remove my space helmet. I will die immediately, one way or another – space is a vacuum. Survival without the spacesuit is impossible. My death could be messy, but, after all, there is nobody to see the mess and nobody will have to clear it up. It will be quick. I have the choice of how and when to die – though not the choice of continued life.

In this reality, I have no need to consider the dragons. I know they are out there, maybe even in the spaceship, but I am out of their reach, far beyond their grasp, lost to them. They may bellow in frustration – I'm not sure whether dragons bellow or roar? Which seems an odd thing to think about when facing imminent death in space, but that's what I am thinking about here, floating further and further away from the Earth. The dragons may make whatever sound they make to express rage and frustration, but they cannot reach me. Nor I them. No point in struggle now.

And if I stay in this reality, I will die very soon now. Do I stay here? Or return, as it seems I can choose to do, to the me who is growing rapidly colder in the waters around what is left of the ice shelf? I am floating, even without a flotation device, and shivering only a little.

I'm not sure I made a definite choice, but here I am, back in the water. Maybe I want at least a small chance of survival? I have some thoughts about the dragons. Perhaps I might be a Dragon Whisperer?

I am so, so cold, though, so lost. Around me is darkness, not even starlight or moonlight visible.

− 6 −

THE SINKING OF THE
TITANIC (1)

Organising the events of a life into a coherent narrative imposes a shape, a pattern, on those events that may not have been apparent at the time. This may be true for everyone's story, but perhaps it is even more true (if anything can be 'truer than true') for someone like my husband, who, within the confines of a single body, appears to have been leading several different lives, experiencing several very different and seemingly incompatible realities. If I stand back from the destructiveness of it, I can almost admire the skill with which he kept his different worlds distinct and separate for years, a lifetime. My head explodes even thinking about the effort involved, yet he made it seem effortless, I realise. He was above all else a consummate actor. Whether or not he had heard of Stanislavski, he was a Method actor, immersing himself in each role, finding the motivation, body language and persona for each separate character. I believed him because he was believable in the roles in which I knew him, and perhaps he was believable because, whilst playing those roles, he believed in them himself. He rarely slipped up. He could ignore all the contradictions and incompatibilities within his different worlds because he simply did not see them, or was somehow able to choose not to see them. At the beginning of this narrative, I was drawn to frame it within a metaphor of the theatre. I realise in this moment that perhaps this owes something to the fact that I lived for more than thirty years with an actor, who was never offstage.

You may have noticed that I have never given my husband a name throughout this story. The name by which I knew him represents a person who did not, in fact, exist and I find it impossible to use that name here. I call him 'my husband' – though he was that in a legal sense only. All else was a role, a game. I don't know what I should call him. Nothing seems appropriate.

His friend comes onstage about now, and he does need a name. In my mind's eye he is not Iago, but a pantomime villain. *He's behind you! Oh, no he isn't.* But oh, yes, he is. What should we call him? Tom, Dick or Harry? Dick, I think. Dick seems to fit him best.

I speculate that perhaps the idea that each of us is a single unified self is something we have to believe in order to get through life, make plans, rear families, build careers. It seems to us, then, that each of us has a core self that is knowable, and that this core self remains to a large extent consistent throughout life. I might say that I am this kind of person or that kind of person. If I am then seen to behave in ways that are completely unlike what is perceived as myself, both I and everyone around me may be distressed, frightened, uncomfortable, even angry. If I am not myself, who am I? Remember King Lear's question – *Who is it who can tell me who I am?* Well, I know who I am, don't I?

Is it possible, though, that this notion of a single core self, travelling in linear fashion from birth to death, is nothing more than a comforting illusion? We may consciously and unconsciously choose, most of the time, to behave and even think in ways that support our notion of our core self, and this maintains the illusion. For someone like my husband, though, who may never have had that sense of a self, of selfness, the internal checks and balances that govern behaviour may operate quite differently, or fail to operate at all. Thus the clergyman, therapist and ethicist, who preaches about the importance of empathy and congruence in personal relationships and 'respect for persons' in all areas of life can simultaneously be the person who humiliates and deceives his wife and family for decades and fucks his internet pick-up in his vicarage. Buffering...

I am hobbled in telling my husband's story because I have no reliable sources of information about his hidden lives. Some of it – the outline – I have been able to piece together from external evidence and careful questioning. ('You ask questions like a barrister would,' he said. 'It's unfair.') But my information comes primarily from three people – my husband, Linda the Un-sister, and my husband's friend Dick. All these people are unreliable narrators and they have all demonstrated their willingness to tell lies. I am not knowingly telling lies here, but I too am an unreliable narrator, seeing events from my own perspective, through my own eyes. And do I sometimes alter things slightly, just to make a better story? Well, yes. The story about the cygnets is true in every detail, right down to the emotions it evoked in me – but it happened not last week but this time last year. There are no cygnets at all this year. Eggs were laid; none hatched. Truth is fluid, many-layered, hard to come by. Memory distorts and rearranges. How do I follow Ariadne's thread through this labyrinth? Is there even a thread to follow?

My husband's view of the truth appeared to be that he had done nothing wrong in using prostitutes and, when that became a little risky, cruising internet dating sites to find women with whom he could have emotional and sexual affairs. (He did not count the emotional affairs as affairs – his relationships only counted as affairs if he actually had sex with the women concerned. Thus his relationship with Linda was not an affair once the sex stopped – because of his prostate problems, just in case you were wondering whether his conscience had troubled him.) He did not 'love' me (*whatever love means...*'), though he did have 'care and concern' for me; he couldn't/didn't want to have sex with me, but wasn't ready to give up his sex life. Of course, he had to use prostitutes or have affairs. What else could he do? It had to be secret because that is the game, because I'd have left if I'd known, and because other people wouldn't understand; he didn't want to lose my family, our dogs, his life as he knew it... Buffering...

This could now become a long and tedious (or longer and more tedious) narrative of who said what, and when and how.

How I did not check my husband's phone for further messages, but did, six weeks later, go through his email account. What I found and how I found it. Speaking to Dick. Speaking to Linda. I will spare all of us a detailed account of how information unfolded, the truths and half-truths, distortions and lies. I can summarise in a few sentences the gist of what the three main protagonists had to say: ·

MY HUSBAND: *I have a dark side – not my fault. It's because of the primal wound of rejection by my birth parents and then the lack of honesty from my adoptive parents. I found out I was adopted in a traumatic and damaging way after the death of my adoptive father when I was eleven. I never had a real father. I have a dark side and have no choice but to follow where it leads me. It makes me 'crap' at personal relationships. I have no choice. Then I am a maverick, a rule breaker... I have to do everything my own way, which has to be different from how other people do things... there is a thrill, a buzz, an adrenalin rush in being different, being transgressive, playing a game. I am 'that lovely man' to so many people, but then there is my dark side, my secrets... And having secrets makes me powerful... I know people might say I've treated you appallingly, but I have a dark side... and I have been faithful for the last three years now. That must count for something... I was entitled to a bit of excitement, after all...*

LINDA: *It was your husband's fault. I am an innocent who found my way on to an internet dating site without realising what it was – silly me! Once I realised what it was, I was intrigued by it, so I had no choice but to stay. I had a difficult* *childhood, and got married too young to a man who couldn't offer me a fulfilling marriage and who had secrets of his own... Your husband pursued me, was desperate for an affair, for love (of a kind). Maybe he just wanted sex, I don't know. But how could I resist? I knew he'd had relationships with other women from the dating site, but I thought I was different. I felt guilty and uncomfortable over the six – Seven? Ten? Thirteen? – years of our affair, but my emotions were involved so I had no choice. He really wanted me to go to your house, walk your dogs, make coffee in your kitchen – how could I resist? I had no choice. But I did feel guilty every time. Honestly. When my husband walked in on us at my house, I had to stop him telling you because it would have been upsetting for you. Your husband and I had to be more careful after that... My marriage ended a few years later – my husband's fault. Neither he nor your husband could give me what I needed, though, so I'm with a widower now, but it was nice to keep in touch with your husband – he was my special person. I deserve to be happy. Sorry about the naked photos, by the way. Not my fault, though – I had no choice. Your husband made it all happen, and I had to go along – you have to when your emotions are involved, after all.*

DICK: *It's the wife's fault. Your poor husband – such a saint. He helped so many people over his lifetime that you were lucky to have him. After all, if he couldn't get along with you, he was entitled to find someone better. I just want him to have a bit of love. If you hadn't been so cold and critical – a bad wife, a bad mother – he wouldn't have been forced into affairs. It's your fault, and you should be grateful that he stayed with you. He and Linda* *sat down in 2012 and decided to carry on as they were, not move in together, so you should appreciate their thought for you. He had to lie – that's part of having affairs – and he couldn't tell the whole truth once you found out about Linda because you wouldn't have liked it. I did tell you he thought a lot about her. Better for him just to lie – and maybe that's all he knew how to do, anyway. He was such a saint, he helped so many people. He had to stay with you because your son disliked you, so your husband had to stay to protect him. I don't know why it's such a big deal – it's only an affair. Well, a few affairs. And a few prostitutes before that. But it's your fault, anyway. I just want him to have a bit of love…*

It seems that here I am allowing each of the protagonists to speak in their own voice. But, of course, whilst I am, as far as possible, using their words, those words have been filtered through me and through the distorting lens of memory. Perhaps what I am conveying is a sense of what it felt like to listen to their words? I can only repeat – buffering…

Am I being cold-hearted, writing the words of each protagonist in this bald, abridged way? It's possible, I suppose – but I'm also trying to spare you some of the sticky, labyrinthine process I experienced as I picked my way through weeks of lies, obfuscations and self-justifications to find my way to something resembling the truth.

My husband had begged me not to leave him. 'I want the truth,' I'd said. 'Full and frank disclosure. One more lie, and I'm gone.'

His first response was to deny everything – not a tenable position, given the text I'd seen. At each point he gave me a story that he thought could explain away the few facts I had, but perhaps, ill as he was, his powers of invention were less efficient than usual. Wearing my Miss Marple hat, I pointed out gaps, inconsistencies and contradictions. Once I found the emails, it was obvious that there was very little truth in anything I'd been told in the six weeks leading up to that point. My husband (and Dick) explained that they only lied to protect me, to save me from painful knowledge – Dick explained this for me. They knew I *believed* I wanted to know the truth, but it was in my best interests (they felt) to be kept in ignorance as far as possible. Writing this now, I'm amazed that I didn't walk away at that point. But my husband was still ill, still in hospital, still needing someone to help advocate for him and plan his discharge… I was still a wife bot. And I felt trapped. 'Please, please don't tell anyone,' my husband said. 'You'll only upset people…' And that, at least, was true… And I, lost in the coldness of their landscape, felt almost paralysed, unable to know my next step.

Reflecting on all this now, I realise how much these two men seem to dislike women, to have no respect for women – maybe to fear them? Listening to some of what they said left me, for once, with no reply. Shocked. Buffering…

Don't forget Dick's justification for all that had happened – my husband couldn't leave because my son disliked me… I don't know if my husband said this to Dick. He certainly never said it to me. Memory, common sense, the responses of my son's closest friends since his death – all these things reassure me that my son did not dislike me. I am left, though, with a tiny inner doubt lurking in a dark cave at the back of my mind. Occasionally it pokes its head out, sniffs the air for prey, sends its forked and sticky tongue flying to hit its defenceless target. And maybe this is what Dick intended?

For the thirty-four years of our marriage, from September 1983 to October 2017, my husband was the *Titanic*, departing Southampton, calling in at Cherbourg in France and Queenstown in Ireland, before heading across the Atlantic towards New York. Like the *Titanic*, my husband went full steam ahead, contemptuous of risk and ignoring iceberg warnings. Why worry about a few icebergs when you are unsinkable?

I suppose years of acting a part, or a whole series of parts, deceiving your family, friends, congregation, the whole world, with seeming ease and without guilt, regret or remorse – no price tag – perhaps all this would make you feel unsinkable?

Here are some clichés. '*The gods punish hubris.*' '*The truth floats up like oil on water.*' '*What goes around, comes around.*' My husband was careless with his phone and his text messages. I wonder if he'd ever seen the film, *A Night to Remember*? There is always an iceberg, looming up suddenly in the darkness.

INTERMISSION

ONCE UPON A TIME... there was a day in a year. And in that day was a minute, a second, an instant – a flash of time. And in that flash of time a decision was made. And that decision grew and spread and appeared to flourish. Over time it became a tree from the deep forest, broad and spreading. An oak tree, perhaps? Or a chestnut?

Its trunk was thick and solid, with rough-textured bark, warm and pleasant and interesting to touch. Children came and made bark rubbings from its surface, paper and crayons pressed against the tree's trunk, pictures becoming trophies to take home to mothers who pinned them to fridges or kitchen walls or else in scrapbooks.

The tree's leaves were green and glossy, all shades merging in greenness, sun reflecting in the shadows of the branches.

In the winter, when the leaves fell to nourish the earth beneath, the brown strength of the branches stood stark against the sky.

In heat and cold, sunshine and blizzards, rain and drought, the tree stood, and it seemed strong and it seemed almost eternal.

But all was not as it seemed to be. The tree's roots, invisible in the earth, were twisted, slimy, rotting. What was beneath, inside the earth, was small, weak, pale, and offered little sustenance to the tree. And yet, above the earth, the tree seemed to flourish. Travellers rested in its shade on hot days. Dog walkers sheltered under its branches when it rained. Strangely, no one noticed that sometimes, very occasionally, a traveller never reached his destination. A dog walker, or a dog, never returned home.

These things happened infrequently and were hidden from view. If the travellers or dog walkers were missed, nobody knew where or how they had vanished. Nobody knew where or how to look for them. Maybe a searching and a sadness continued. They were never found.

And days and nights went by. The years turned. People passed by and admired the tree, its colours, its solidity, its strength. Lives came and went. Days passed, and years. The tree remained. Children still came to make bark rubbings, as their parents had done and, as well as bark rubbings, most of them also made good memories. One or two of them, though, would go to bed and have troubling dreams, feeling trapped in a cage of green leaves. This didn't happen often, and the troubling dreams were, perhaps, the product of too much sunshine and an over-busy day.

And then, one night, there came a great storm that roared through the country, intent on destruction. The storm had built its strength far out to sea, huge energies sucked up from the ocean and down from the sky, boiling, whirling and howling over the land.

The next day dawned cold and grey. People who had huddled in their houses through the night, praying for the storm to pass, went out to survey the damage and count the dead. Loss, destruction and sadness were over the land. People wept, and then began to repair what could be repaired, save who could be saved and clear away whatever was beyond repair or saving.

At first nobody noticed that the tree no longer stood. And then, a little boy, searching for his lost cat, heard her meowing, found her, unharmed, but trapped in the tree by the fallen canopy of the leaves. He rescued the kitty, and went home and told his mother what he had seen.

People came to view the fallen tree. They saw the strong-seeming trunk, now sideways on the ground, the glossy green leaves and the branches all twisted and broken. And they saw the roots, dragged from the earth – not big and strong as the tree had seemed but grey and fungoid and rotten, twisted and small. How had the tree survived so long with such weak roots? Then someone noticed shapes, skulls, some human, caught in the tangled slime of the roots, trapped.

And they could not comprehend what they saw.

– 7 –

THOUGHTS AND FEELINGS
ARE THOUGHTS AND
FEELINGS...

They are not facts. What has happened to my other self who is revolving slowly, weightless, drifting further and further into deep space?

I am, I realise, a disembodied consciousness, no longer experiencing myself inside the spacesuit. Now I am floating – bodiless, so safe – in the vacuum of space. The spacesuit is over there, I see, still turning, still moving away... I see my dead self inside the spacesuit, my helmet half off – maybe there wasn't time to remove it completely? I avoid looking too closely at what remains. It seems I chose the swift and immediate death. And yet I am still here, observing, noticing.

So despite the damaged helmet, the vacuum of space, the deep, deep cold, I am not dead. I am, in fact, alive.

I decide to try an experiment. Effortlessly, I take myself

back into the frozen waters. Enough of this now. I need to be on the land. And as all of this is just the product of thoughts and feelings, and is not a fact – here I am – on the land. I can see rocks and ice dimly in the darkness – no sign of life. Think. What do I need? A hypothermia blanket, dry clothes, a fur-lined parka, a flask of something lukewarm to drink – not caffeine, not alcohol and nothing too hot. It might be dangerous to raise my body temperature too quickly. I think again. What else do I need? Some high-energy food – bread, peanut butter, sugary biscuits. Drink a little, eat a little, move a little. Put on the dry clothes quickly, and then the fur-lined parka. I momentarily enjoy the soft luxuriousness of the fur lining – not cruel vanity, this, but a necessity in the freezing temperatures. Drink a little, eat a little, move a little. Do a few star jumps. Warm up slowly and carefully.

The darkness seems to be lifting. Soon it will be daylight. The icy landscape fades and I find myself walking in endless grassland, green in every direction. Perhaps I feel some green thoughts beginning to sprout in my mind? There is only greenness – greenitude? Is that a word? Long grasses waving gently in a warm and pleasant breeze. I begin to walk, feeling the sun on my back. Time to ditch the fur-lined parka, I think, and there it is – gone. I continue to walk up a gentle slope. Somewhere ahead of me, or behind me or to the side of me, are the dragons, still here, still waiting. Could I make them visible? I decide not to try. Not just yet.

Do I see movement ahead of me? Something fluttering? Colour? As I reach the top of the slope, I see in the hollow beneath me a bright, stripy circus tent, a big top – flags flying, people streaming in, noise, chattering, music. The circus is about to begin. I need to hurry – I'm in it!

I can't remember when I last went to the circus. My mind flips back to a memory six decades old. I am eight, and someone has taken me to Blackpool Tower Circus. We are sitting by the ringside, only a couple of rows back. I have been to this circus before, and I know we are at the point where the spotlight will settle on a little girl in the audience, all other lights will dim, and world-famous clown Charlie Cairoli, standing in the same beam of light, will sing 'Thank Heaven For Little Girls', singing directly to the child in the spotlight. I have always felt relieved that the spotlight did not settle on me. I am a quiet, noticing child, with no desire to sit in a spotlight being sung to by a clown whilst hundreds of people watch.

But this time I am that child, caught in the spotlight I didn't choose. I feel myself becoming one big blush, red all over. I remember with immediacy shrinking in my seat, feeling slightly pleased but mostly excruciatingly embarrassed. I am glad when Charlie finishes singing and there is something else for people to look at.

I don't think that is the last time I went to a circus, though. Did we ever take my son to a circus? I really can't remember. I need to remember. I can't remember. I have no one to ask. I hope my son went to a circus at least once. But I can't remember.

I still need to hurry. I can hear the opening music start up and the clowns are on in a few minutes. I look down at my feet and see my enormous bright orange clown shoes. No wonder I can't run. I look down at my clothes – the bright, garish costume of the Auguste clown. I reach up and feel my round red nose. This won't do. Think again. And now I am a White-faced Clown, like Charlie Cairoli's Paul, wearing shoes that allow me to run. The White-faced Clown is, of course, the archetypal clown whose mask hides heartbreak. But the show must go on…

And here I am, in the Big Top, back in my Auguste outfit, I see. So I play my role – it's strange, but I know what to do, almost as if I had rehearsed this. So I run round, chased by the other clowns. They rip off my baggy pants, trip me up, shove gloopy custard pies in my face, and all the time the audience roars with laughter. My role in this troupe of clowns seems to be to play the stupid one, the butt of the jokes, the prat who takes the pratfall, all for the amusement of the crowd. Timing is everything. I need to be in the right place to take the custard pie in the face every time, while seeming to stumble about foolishly and without direction. How well I know my steps. We work together skilfully, my fellow clowns and I, and the audience loves us.

And here we are in the Big Parade at the end of the show, dancing around the ring with the elephants, jugglers and acrobats, following the top-hatted ringmaster in his bright red coat, alternately waving to the people in the audience and then teasing them, pretending to throw a bucket of water over them – but of course it is just shiny shredded paper, glitter and tinsel. We throw sweets to the children. Everyone loves us.

The show is over. People go home, all the excited children, the exhausted parents. The Big Top becomes quiet and still as darkness falls. Time to go to my caravan and take off my make-up, red nose, orange wig, and all. Maybe the White-faced Clown and I can sit down together for half an hour and enjoy a small glass of Laphroaig and swop stories about hurt, and pain and loss. We are both clichés, after all – clowns who are crying inside. I need to guard against self-pity here. It won't help.

Let's get biblical for a moment – after all, I was married to a clergyman. *'Is it nothing to you, all ye that pass by? Behold and see if there be any sorrow like unto my sorrow, which is close to me...'* (Lamentations 1:12). And then the closing words of the Book of Lamentations: *'Turn thou us unto thee, O Lord, and we shall be turned; renew our days as of old. But thou hast utterly rejected us; thou art very wroth against us...'* (Lamentations 5: 21–22). I remember too the words of Job's wife in the Book of Job, that most puzzling of books in the Bible. As God heaps tribulations on to the head of Job and his family to test Job's faith, Job's wife reaches the end of her tether: *'Curse God and die...'* (Job 2:9). I have had the same thought myself. It's very tempting.

And yet is it really so simple? The problem of suffering has defeated philosophers and theologians over centuries. If God/Goddess is all-knowing and all-powerful, why does he/she allow good people to suffer? But is it all more random than that? No simple cause and effect? No simple equations that if we are good, good things will happen and if we transgress, we will get our comeuppance? Yet another cliché – *life isn't fair.* Simple as that. *Why me?* Why not me, after all? Maybe sometimes things just happen the way they happen because that's the way they happen.

I can see with hindsight a pattern to my life, things I could and maybe should have done to save myself and my son. But that's hindsight for you. It isn't foresight. I was doing my best at the time, in the light of the information available to me. Maybe we are here, floating on our space rock, and we just have to get on with it as best we can. Staying with the Bible for one more moment, I find in Matthew 5:45: '*God causes his sun to rise on the evil and the good, and sends rain on the righteous and unrighteous.*' There are many sorrows like unto my sorrow, now and through all time. I am not alone or special in sorrow. We all experience happiness and we all suffer. Everybody who lives or has ever lived knows sorrow like unto my sorrow, one way or another.

Everything that can happen to me has happened before in one way or another to someone else, and will happen again many times to other people. As I have a place in the line of grieving mothers, so I have a place in the line of betrayed wives, and all the other lines of people who have made unwise choices, been duped, or duped themselves. But there are other lines too. Not all the choices were unwise so I also belong in the line of people who chose well. I have met people who are honest, whose care for others is REALLY real, who are real Polar Bears. Maybe I can have a place in their line, even if only on the substitute's bench? Everything is transient. Everyone experiences happiness and suffering, and both are inextricably part of life. Maybe we just have to stop blaming God, if there is such a being, stop expecting rescue or reason, and just embrace life in all its complexity... (*I can't decide whether to end that last sentence with a full stop or with a question mark. You choose.)*

When I was young, my mother often used to quote the poet John Gay (1685–1732). He composed his own epitaph, which is engraved upon his tomb in Poets' Corner in Westminster Abbey:

> *Life's a jest and all things show it;*
> *I thought so once, and now I know it.*

I find this a comforting thought.*

And now maybe the White-faced Clown and I can have one more tiny glass of Laphroaig before it is time to go to sleep.

*I wanted to be sure that I was quoting John Gay's epitaph correctly, so looked it up online. I find that he also wrote, 'The comfortable estate of widowhood is the only hope that keeps up a wife's spirits.' *Cruel, perhaps, but it made me laugh.*

− 8 −

ON THE IMPORTANCE
OF NAMES

Names have traditionally been held to carry power. There have, for example, been many traditional beliefs in different parts of the country about the naming of new babies. A common theme was the belief that once the parents have chosen a name, they should keep it to themselves and their immediate family until the baby has been christened. This is to prevent harmful or malevolent entities using knowledge of the child's name to gain power or cause damage before the child has been protected by Christian baptism.

One piece of traditional wisdom that I wish I'd known thirty-five years ago is the belief that it is unlucky for a woman to marry a man whose last name begins with the same letter as her maiden name:

Change the name and not the letter,
Change for the worse and not for the better…

So once again I learn something when it is too late for it to be of much use to me…

Within many cultures throughout history, there have been beliefs and customs around the importance of your true name. In some cultures, for example, it has been considered wise to be known by a nickname, to prevent witches from using your true name in spells and charms that might be harmful. Keeping your true name secret helps to keep you safe.

Names are important. Names have power.

I said earlier that I have found it impossible to use my husband's given name here because the person I knew by that name did not exist, and so is nameless. I have called him 'my husband' throughout, but this is wrong too. The phrase 'my husband' carries implications about relationship, closeness, mutual care. Perhaps even some mutual honesty and respect? I don't feel like a wife. It occurs to me now to wonder how long this has been true, though mostly unacknowledged? Some years ago, one of my dogs and I were attacked by another dog in the park. My dog was bruised and terrified, but otherwise uninjured. My left hand was bitten, and I had to go to hospital to have the wound cleaned and stitched. The nurse said it was necessary to cut off my wedding ring. I protested. 'I can cut it off now,' she said, 'or you can come back in the middle of the night when your hand is swollen and you are in agony, and we will cut it off then.' Off it came.

I never had it repaired, so wore no wedding ring. A year or two later, my husband bought me a replacement, largely at the urging of a silversmith whose studio we were visiting. I have rarely worn it, and even more rarely worn it on my wedding finger. It no longer fits well and I've worried about losing it. It's a nice ring. I might give it to one of my nieces.

In recent days, a strange thing has been happening, and it is happening with increasing frequency. My hands and wrists are often clumsily painful and painfully clumsy – there are good reasons, rooted in my physical health, for this to be so. But I'm finding that the pain intensifies when I write, or even type the words, 'my husband'. This doesn't happen every time; sometimes (less frequently) my hands start to shake, and sometimes I just feel sick – though I have not, to date, needed to clean up any more vomit from my kitchen floor. For this small mercy, I am thankful.

My body is telling me that I need to give my husband a name, but it has to be a new name, to acknowledge a new reality. I've decided to call him 'Lovely Donald'. I'll explain the 'Lovely' bit later; maybe you can figure out the 'Donald' bit for yourself? (Answers on a postcard, please.)

In fact, we need to sort out this name thing once and for all. So – my husband is 'Lovely Donald'. His friend remains 'Dick'. 'Linda' is herself, of course, and I'm using her true name. I wonder if I am a malevolent entity wanting some kind of power over her? But I'm also using her name – Linda – generically, to stand for all the unknown women with whom Lovely Donald enjoyed hidden relationships over the course of our marriage. In changing my husband's name – part of his identity – and that of his friend, am I exercising a kind of power over them? They do not know I am doing this, and so cannot give consent.

Am I, in a smaller way, doing to them what they did to me? Changing their identity? Manipulating it to suit myself? Is this a kind of minor revenge? I don't think so. I hope not. I know that I have to be vigilant, to guard against revenge. Like self-pity, it won't help. Maybe I'm remembering an old phrase that used to be used in dramatisations of true events – 'the names have been changed to protect the innocent'. Or something like that.

And what should you call me? Goodness, I don't know. If you know my true name, might that give you power over me? I remember all the myths, legends and fairy stories that tell us of the power of names. Maybe you can call me Rumpelstiltskin? You think that's a bit too cumbersome? A bit of a silly name? Okay – well, you can call me 'Hattie' then. It's not my name, but it will serve. I'll answer to it.

My painful, shaking hands have led me to reflect on the ways in which emotion can be manifested physically in the body in complex ways.

Lovely Donald and Linda, in creating for themselves some shared experiences and shared memories, have stolen all my memories of my marriage and even some of my memories of my son's childhood. I no longer know what, if anything, was real or true. (Whatever reality or truth might be.) When we were visiting the Black House on Skye or walking up Glastonbury Tor or going to the Natural History Museum or Blackpool Tower, we were a family, enjoying ourselves… I believed. In all the day-to-day mundanity of meals, work, school, dog walking, bedtimes, arguments, laughter, I still believed that we were a family. What was Lovely Donald's experience, though? Was he just waiting for the day to be over so he could 'reach out' to the Linda of the moment? What was my son's experience? Was he aware on any level, conscious or unconscious, of the emotional dishonesty that permeated our home, our lives? What effect might that have had on him over the years? My head aches at the thought of all these competing and conflicting realities and complexities. My muscles tense. There is no stable or secure ground on which I can stand. I am in danger of losing my balance. (The Laphroaig probably isn't helping.)

My son. He was in every way himself. Sir Murf. He became Murf very early in his life – a nickname drawn from his initials. He always loved tales of knights and dragons, and as he grew into his late teens, enjoyed dressing up in armour and re-enacting medieval battles. And so – Sir Murf. I see him in his life, as he was at all the ages he reached – not so many, really. He is standing at the back gate in his long leather coat, his dreadlocks hanging down his back. Is he coming in or going out? I feel a stab of pain, a knife, narrowly missing a vital spot; so I carry on living, just about, more or less. Then there is the almost constant cold, damp heaviness, greyness, in my chest, weighty, restricting my breathing. Sometimes it feels heavier, damper, colder and I find it difficult to breathe at all. At other times it feels a little lighter. It never goes away.

HIATUS

I focus on my breathing, following the breath into my body and out of my body... I pay attention to the physical sensations of the in-breath, my body expanding with the inflow of oxygen. I notice, too, the physical sensations of the out-breath, my chest and abdomen subsiding as the air leaves my body. My breath rises and falls, rises and falls, like the movement of the tide flowing up and down the beach...

I notice any areas of pain or stiffness or discomfort in my body, letting go of any feeling of resistance to my experience in the moment... I breath gently into those areas of pain and tension, soothing and softening them. The breath flows in... and the breath flows out. I am here, now, breathing...

I seek out any pleasant sensations in my body right now... Perhaps my hands don't hurt quite so much at this moment as they did earlier? I can feel a cool breeze from the open window gently soothing my face. I become aware of the weight of my dog, lying across my feet, gently snoring. I smile.

Breathe in...

Breathe out...

Now I take a moment or two to rest in the wholeness of my breath, my body swelling and subsiding. I can feel the air around my nostrils as it enters my body… I feel the movement of the air in my chest and abdomen. Do I feel some movement of air in my back? My body expands as the air flows in, and subsides with the warmer air leaving my body as I breathe out through my mouth…

Thoughts, feelings and images constantly come into my mind, meandering or racing according to their nature. I don't need to hang on to them or follow them… I let them in, the thoughts and feelings, observe them for a moment – and then let them go, like clouds in the sky, floating away.

Breathing in…

Breathing out…

Following my breath…

And after a few minutes of this, I can focus on the chair beneath me, my feet on the floor. My mind is less restless, my body less tense. This won't last forever, but for now I can pick up my pen and continue to write.

– 9 –

SEND OUT THE CLOWNS?

I don't think I like being a clown. I don't like being a stereotype, either – a clown hiding heartbreak behind a painted smile, a betrayed wife. I seem to be stuck in the costume of the White-faced Clown; I can't switch back into the Auguste outfit as I could before. I've experienced the performance as an Auguste clown, so now, in order to be allowed to leave the circus behind, perhaps I have to go through the performance again, but this time from the perspective of a very different kind of clown. I really, really want to leave the circus, so I am not arguing or struggling. If this is what I have to do in order to get away from here, then I will do it.

Clowns are jolly; clowns are fun. But clowns can be sinister and frightening too. *Coulrophobia*: perhaps this is an internet-generated word rather than a true medical or psychiatric diagnosis? It means a morbid fear of clowns.

My sister, who at forty had a savage dying but a peaceful death, collected clowns. We will return to my sister and her death later, but for now I am remembering her room, full of models, pictures, soft toys, images – clowns in every shape you can imagine, and possibly some that would never occur to you. I don't have a morbid fear of clowns, but, I have to say, being in her room, clowns wherever the eye alighted, did slightly give me the creeps.

So I didn't particularly like being in the garish clown outfit of yesterday, and I like today's White-faced Clown costume even less. I'll wear it, for now.

I'm backstage for the moment, but I can hear the opening bars of the music. The performance is about to begin. We prepare to make our entrance…

Thank God, it is over. The audience is leaving. The stagehands are out in the Big Top, clearing up the elephant dung and all the other detritus of the performance.

My fellow clowns and I put on exactly the same act as yesterday, but my experience, as the White-faced Clown, not the Auguste, was utterly different.

The world of the clowns seems anarchic, chaotic, the world turned upside down. Yet I have learned over the last two performances how carefully scripted and choreographed the act has to be if it is to work. Each clown has to know exactly what to do and how and when to do it to make it all look spontaneous and natural. But in reality it is very carefully constructed, as it has to be. Timing is everything.

Nothing is as it seems in the world of the clowns. On the face of it, the White- faced Clown enjoys higher status than the Augustes, acting as a kind of referee or ringmaster – on the face of it. He is the straight man and, as is so often the case with the straight man in a comedy act, he is ripe for ridicule and humiliation. He appears to have authority, or at least to believe that he has authority, but all the time the Augustes are subtly belittling and undermining him – and this is where the comedy lies. The White-faced Clown thinks he is clever; the Augustes are bumbling idiots. But in fact perhaps the Augustes are like the Trickster or Joker of mythology and Batman movies – cleverer than they look. The White-faced Clown falls for it every time.

I realise that I have always been uncomfortable with clowns, and that this is not just because Charlie Cairoli put me in a spotlight and sang to me when I was eight. The pratfalls, the playing with reality – this feels like the comedy of humiliation, and I'm not sure that I find other people's humiliation funny, even when they offer themselves up for it. Maybe this explains my discomfort with some types of reality TV and the excesses of celebrity culture? This may be a defect in me – maybe I am too serious, have less of a sense of humour than I think I do. I don't know; that's how I feel.

Lovely Donald believed, or at least stated, that as long as I didn't know of his hidden life, no harm was being done to me. This reminds me of the ancient riddle about the tree that falls in a forest. If a tree falls in a forest and there is nobody to hear it, does it make a sound? It's a question with many answers, and you will be drawn to the answer that best reflects you, your personality, your beliefs. If you are being humiliated but you don't know it is happening, are you still being humiliated?

Actually, it's not quite like the tree, is it? There was someone to hear it fall, to hear the sound of my humiliation, even though it wasn't me. Lovely Donald, Linda and Friend Dick all heard the sound of my humiliation. So does that make it real? Lovely Donald did not delete his text messages or his emails or his web-browsing history. As I have sorted through his Himalayan paper mountain since his death, I have found the sad naked photographs and 'I love you' cards (addressed to a PO Box number) hidden in a box file marked 'Sermons'. Perhaps he thought he was immortal and there would always be time to tidy all this away; perhaps he thought he wanted to leave some little booby traps for people to trip over after his death; perhaps he didn't think at all.

Thoughts and feelings are thoughts and feelings; they are not facts. Here I am, still dressed as a White-faced Clown. I could free myself from the Clown costume in an instant, just by thinking myself into the next phase of the multiverse. That feels wrong, though. I need to take some time to divest myself of this outfit, to remove the make-up carefully and thoroughly, to take off the costume, fold it up and put it away. I need a ritual for this ending.

I know the dragons are closer now, though I am still not quite ready for them to be fully visible. I am aware of them, can see a thickening of the air in my peripheral vision that I know is them. But there is more I need to learn before I actually meet them.

– 10 –

THE SINKING OF
THE *TITANIC* (2)

Titanic – a name with resonance, even now, more than a hundred years after the convergence with the iceberg that took both the ship and some 1,500 people to the bottom of the deep Atlantic. There it remains, gradually becoming a part of the seabed, dissolving into the ocean – 15 April 1912; a night to remember.

I think that most people know two things about the *Titanic*:

It was unsinkable.

It sank.

The name *Titanic* derives from Greek mythology. The Titans were a race of giants who aspired to rule heaven. They were defeated and supplanted by the family of Zeus, though, and their giant size did not save them.

Lovely Donald was, like the Titans, larger than life in many ways. He was a big man, physically – he was over six feet tall, and he struggled all his life with his weight. He had a big appetite – for food, for drink, for sex (up to a point) and, it seemed, for life – though maybe this proved to be illusory. He cast a big shadow. When I went to collect his ashes from the funeral director – the same one who managed my son's funeral – the staff there insisted on carrying Lovely Donald's casket out to my car. They seemed convinced that, even as ashes, he was too heavy for me to carry. I wonder what symbolism lay in the fact that it was two women who carried him out for me?

It used to surprise me sometimes – often – how Lovely Donald got through life, cheerfully ignoring the rules and norms of behaviour that most of us have to respect or face negative consequences. He had a charm, a charisma, that meant that people liked him, laughed with him, treated him indulgently and allowed him to 'do it his way'. Maybe there was a childlike quality about him too that led people to want to take care of him, help him. People forgave him, even when doing it his way caused them inconvenience or wasted time. There were few dissenters from the chorus of praise for Lovely Donald, and they tended to be regarded as humourless killjoys. I might, very occasionally, have been a bit of a humourless killjoy myself; I sometimes felt that in doing things his way, Lovely Donald treated other people with disregard and disrespect. Sometimes I tried to mitigate the negative consequences or prompt him into being a bit more considerate; I rarely got any thanks. 'It's all right – that's just Donald. He's such a lovely man… so kind…'

Maybe this was when I morphed into the cold, harsh and critical shrew that I became for him? I might remind him that this prospective bride has already left five increasingly anxious messages about her wedding, and suggest he ring her back before she left a sixth. Or I might remind him that the registrar in our local town had now rung every day for a week, pleading for the all-important green forms that she needed in order to complete her monthly returns. 'They aren't important,' said Lovely Donald. 'I'll do them when I'm good and ready.' They were important to the registrar, though – 'Yes,' says Lovely Donald, 'but those are her priorities, not mine.' Likewise the bride – 'She is just being overanxious. I'll ring her when I'm ready.' I doubted myself and my perceptions. 'He's such a lovely man.' 'He's so humble and authentic.' 'He's helped us so much.' 'Maybe he's crap at the admin but he gets all the important bits right.' 'We're lucky to have him.' 'You're lucky to have him –' often followed quickly with – 'and he's lucky to have you too, of course.' 'You two make such a good team.' 'Lovely Donald.' 'Lovely Donald.' 'Lovely Donald.' I'm amazed he had time for a secret life – the life we all knew about seemed more than busy enough. Like everyone else, I made lots of allowances for Lovely Donald, though my frustration did occasionally creep out, or even roar out. These were small things in the loveliness of Donald, though and, after all, none of us is perfect. Sometimes someone would say, 'Donald is so lovely but I can imagine he might be hard work to live with.' I used to smile. I occasionally heard the gentle tinkling of little warning bells in my head, but I dismissed them. They tinkled gently but insistently over the years, but it was never really clear what they were warning me about. I dismissed them again – and again. I trusted in the wisdom of the crowd around us, Donald admirers all . And I don't think I'm that easy to live with myself.

There was bad stuff out there, but maybe there was good stuff too? This good stuff was also part of Lovely Donald – I think. It is indisputable that he appeared to help people and they felt helped. I go round in circles asking myself whether his dishonesty, hypocrisy and lack of care or respect for me and his family undermines the good stuff, makes it inauthentic. I don't reach any conclusions. Actually, that's not true. I reach a conclusion every day – but then I reach the opposite conclusion tomorrow. I think I have to tick the 'don't know' box.

It all looks different now – with hindsight, of course. At the time, whilst this marriage lacked (for me) intimacy and sharing, my life was not awful; there were (I thought) some good times, and we were moving forward in our shared enterprise with shared values. My marriage was a compromise – like the marriages of most of the women I knew. There's a saying – '*What you don't know can't hurt you.*' My son would have called that saying 'a crock of shit'. What you don't know can hurt you beyond healing.

Many, many people have said to me in the months since Donald's death – I did tell you he died, didn't I? – 'Donald was such a lovely man. You must be lost without him.' Usually I just smile and say nothing. I'm not lost without him. I think I was lost with him.

The *Titanic* was considered to be unsinkable because of its sixteen watertight compartments extending above the waterline. These compartments could be sealed off with watertight doors if, God forbid, there was an emergency. Nobody seems to have realised until too late that this was true only up to a certain point. One, or two or three or four of the watertight compartments could be flooded and the ship would survive. The particular combination of circumstances on the night of 15 April 1912 meant that the iceberg tore a jagged hole along the side of the ship. Five compartments were flooded. The ship was doomed. 'Unsinkable' doesn't really mean *unsinkable*. It just means that the ship probably won't sink unless something very unlikely happens. Nothing is perfect. Unusual and unlikely things do happen – on the *Titanic*'s maiden voyage and at the end of Lovely Donald's life.

Lovely Donald always said that he needed to keep the various aspects of his life in watertight compartments. He likened himself to a roast dinner – everything distinct and separate on the plate, with maybe some gravy to bring it all together. I, on the other hand, he said, was a stew (or did he say 'shrew'?) or a casserole – everything all mixed up together, flavours merging and melding to combine a whole. All part of 'life's great rich tapestry' – or should I say life's great rich smorgasbord? We are all different. Funnily enough, I prefer casseroles to roast dinners. Lovely Donald preferred blisteringly hot curries to either*. His 'roast dinner-ness' used to frustrate me sometimes – but then my 'casserole-ness' used to frustrate him too. Give and take, compromise – all part of married life. At least in my universe.

I saw the exact moment when Lovely Donald's watertight

---

* *Perhaps the Lindas resembled a Vindaloo? Or even a phall?*

compartments flooded, and the exact moment when he realised that too many of them had gone for him to remain seaworthy. 'The convergence of the twain', as Thomas Hardy called it. The moment when the ship and iceberg came together in a way that Hardy seems to suggest was somehow predestined, an inevitable clash between human technology and the forces of nature. '*And as the smart ship grew/ In stature, grace and hue/ In shadowy silent distance grew the iceberg too.*' Perhaps Donald's meeting with his iceberg, was also predestined. After all, he had handed me his phone and asked me to look at it to find a number. How did it come about that a message from 2014 was there in front of me? I came across a saying around this time – '*The truth floats up like oil on water.*' I may have quoted it before. Secrets, often toxic in their effects even on their keeper, are very hard to keep. Is it possible that secrets sometimes refuse to be kept?

I gave Lovely Donald his phone back a couple of days later, after Oliver – remember him? – had told me that the doctors were now much more optimistic about Donald's prognosis. He was doing pretty well.

When Oliver left, I handed Lovely Donald his phone, and told him that there was at least one message on it that he probably hadn't wanted me to see and certainly would not want his sons to see. He might, I suggested calmly, be wise to delete it, along with any other similar messages.

Lovely Donald looked bewildered. 'I don't know what you are talking about.' There was nothing on his phone that he wouldn't want people to see. Perhaps he is in the situation of the lookout in the crow's nest on the *Titanic*. He sees the iceberg approaching, huge and threatening, but it is already too late to avoid it. He is beginning to see, perhaps, that a collision is inevitable. And now, with a grinding sound of tearing metal, the collision comes.

'There is a message on your phone from a woman called Linda, who is not your sister. She wishes you were in bed together so she could kiss you all over. She misses her lollipop.'

Lovely Donald said nothing. He took the phone, turning it over and over in his hands, staring at it in silence. The iceberg moves on. Its work here is done.

Other visitors arrive. We talk of other things. A nurse comes to check Donald's monitors. I leave – I need to go home and walk the dogs.

I am about to get biblical again. Don't worry – it won't matter if you skip this next bit if you prefer. I won't be offended. Numbers 32:23: '*… and be sure your sin will find you out*'.

This sounds like another way of saying, '*the truth floats up like oil on water*', but it is perhaps saying something slightly different. In Donald's case the 'sin' might be less the extramarital sex – hardly unusual – but more the deceit, the living a double life, pretending to be one person while behaving as another. Dr Jekyll and Mr Hyde. Deacon Brodie. The disparity between his two personas was huge, unfathomable, incomprehensible.

Although he later said he felt no guilt either at the time or after he realised I knew about Linda, and that he had enjoyed both the sex and the deception, nonetheless all this pretence does require effort, premeditation and planning.

Also a willingness to spend time with people who trust you, love you, consider you part of their family, whilst knowing all the time that you are not the person they think you are. Knowing that you are deceiving not only your wife, but everyone you claim to care about. I wonder whether, as the years go by, all of this has a corrosive effect from the inside out? Your sin will find YOU out. Lovely Donald did not age well, and perhaps the act became harder to sustain. Perhaps the inner smallness, the inner darkness, begins to show itself externally, in small ways initially, but becoming harder and harder to contain. The watertight compartments are no longer watertight. I have wondered whether Lovely Donald, perhaps at some level outside his conscious awareness, was tired, was wanting to bring an end to all this when he handed me his phone. I wondered whether I sensed a weariness in him, a kind of realisation that in betraying his family he had also betrayed himself, the person he was capable of being. The real 'Lovely Donald'. As he moved slowly but inexorably towards the end of his life, perhaps he had the opportunity for redemption of a kind. He didn't want me to leave, he said. I wasn't sure what was possible. We had much shared history and much shared sadness. Donald was going to need help after discharge from hospital and who would provide it, if not me? But I did know that in order for me to be able to even consider staying with him, I needed total honesty now. It might have happened that way, in some corner of the multiverse.

– 11 –

BEAM ME UP, SCOTTY...

The circus has moved on. The clowns looked for me for a while, but I made sure they didn't find me. The Ringmaster shrugged his shoulders and said it was time to leave. The clowns, unrecognisable out of uniform, left me behind. I have wiped away the clown make-up and packed away the costumes. The inner sadness is much more difficult to remove. And I've just noticed that the White-faced Clown has nicked off with the rest of my Laphroaig – bastard. The dragons roar in the far-off distance but it is not yet their time.

Questions. Am I so unlovable, so unlikeable, so worthless? What is wrong with me that my husband, my son's father, the good, caring and ethically aware Lovely Donald, can treat me with such contempt and disrespect over so many years? And say he enjoyed doing so? What is it about me, what I do, who I am, that allowed this to happen? Asked so few questions? Made so few demands? I realise that I might be asking the wrong question here, of course – perhaps I should be asking not what is wrong with me but what was wrong with him? There is something to be explored here, though – what in me kept me in this situation, ignoring all my little warning bells? What in me got me into this situation in the first place? It is easy to say it's all Donald's fault; but I am not innocent. Maybe I need to look at myself too. That will come later, though. For now I keep returning to my first thought. Am I really so worthless?

It has crossed my mind that Lovely Donald, knowing very well the high value I give to honesty, with myself and with other people, was actively trying to harm me over these years. As I've sorted out the stuff mountain he hoarded over his life, there have, as I mentioned earlier, been a couple of little IEDs, improvised explosive devices that went off when I stepped unwarily. One way or another, I would have learned about his secret life. But the understanding comes that in order to have a desire to harm someone, you have to have an awareness of that person, some powerful emotion towards them. They have to matter enough to you to generate the desire to cause harm. Lovely Donald was never actively trying to harm me. He simply did not see me as a separate human being, with my own worth, my own feelings and needs. I became an adjunct, useful enough in a practical sense and providing what MI5 might call 'deep cover' for his clergyman-and-good-guy self. Me being me was what enabled him to be him. Towards the very end of his life he sometimes confused me with his first wife and seemed unsure which of us was with him on the hospital ward. I began to understand that we were both actually just screens on to which he could project his complex and negative feelings about women, mothers, people who let you down. 'Wives,' he said to a friend, 'are hard to please.' But he never really tried very hard to please either of us, and he presented us both to other people as being critical, judgemental, cold, unloving and harsh. I don't recognise either of us in that description, but maybe that was how he experienced us through the filter of his own personality and past life. Perhaps in some ways we were both his creations. Confusingly, though, he said other things at other times to other people, giving me high praise (which he couldn't have known I'd ever see). Maybe what he said, how he felt, depended on who was in charge at that moment – Dr Jekyll or Mr Hyde. Lovely Donald or his rather less lovely alter ego.

The landscape has shifted again. I am pressed down by an oppressive heat. Sweat soaks my clothes, runs down my face. I can taste its warm, oily saltiness. The air is moist, heavy. It is hard to move, almost like trying to walk chest-deep in water. I can barely move or breathe.

I am walking, barefoot, in a jungle – dense, impenetrable foliage all around me. Rustlings. Birdsong. Insect noises. Screams or screeches – animal? Human? I am not safe here. I have no machete, no backpack, no water, no shoes, no protection. I have no idea where I am. I have no idea where or how to find other people. I am alone and lost in a jungle – but which jungle? Which country? I feel a sensation, look down. Leeches have fastened on to my bare legs and are growing fat on my blood. I remember from somewhere that I can't just knock them off because of the risk of infection. I can't bear to touch them, anyway. They are touching me. More of them, on my arms now. I could die here. I have no direction to go in.

I really cannot do this any more. I am too old, too tired, too ill, too pressed down, pressed back, crushed by the weight of the airless air. I really cannot do this. I want my life back. I want my child.

– 12 –

'SHE MUST HAVE KNOWN SOMETHING...'

Are you still with me? Still reading? If you are, I imagine that there might be two thoughts swirling around for you:

1. She must have known *something*...
2. For heaven's sake, what's the big deal? Man has affairs. Man lies to wife and family. This happens every bloody day – nothing titanic about it. All right, vicar uses prostitutes, goes to online dating sites to find a co-adulterer, leads a double life for at least eighteen years – maybe that's a bit more out of the ordinary. Even so, is it really worth 20,966 words?

Are you bored? Do you think I should just shut up, stop going on about it all and get on with what little life I have left? I've certainly thought that from time to time. It's possible I'm even boring myself.

Let's take the second point first. I do like to do things in the wrong order. Maybe I have more in common with Lovely Donald than I think. A sudden insistent image flashes into my mind. Lovely Donald and me, gin and tonics in our hands (and it's obvious that we've already had a few), singing in raucous imitation of Frank Sinatra, '*I did it my-y-y-y-y-y-y-y-y way!*' Trust me, it never happened. '*Regrets, I've had a few...*' Stop.

So, what's the big deal? Extramarital sex. So far, so ordinary. That's not really what I'm writing about here, and nor is that the greatest betrayal in my eyes. Linda is irrelevant in a weird way. If it hadn't been her, it would have been someone else. In fact, it was someone else before her and maybe even alongside her. I wouldn't waste 21,000 words on Lovely Donald's need for a transgressive, secret sex life and some emotionally charged pen-pal relationships. What I am writing about is my own life, how it feels to have my life as I knew it disappear, in a second. Pop! It's gone. Now you see it, now you don't. How it feels to discover in a moment that I was married for thirty-four years not to the person I thought I was married to but a total stranger. After thirty-four years, I met someone I didn't recognise and didn't much like. Something formless and shapeless took form and shape. Someone larger than life became small, twisted and Gollum-like. I heard the voice of the addict – 'my precioussssss'. Just as my life went 'pop!', so the Lovely Donald we all knew, loved and trusted went 'pop!' too. He never existed. His 'Lovely Donald' face was only a mask of integrity and caring, a 'good man face' to hide behind, like the sad person hiding behind the clown make-up.

Equally importantly, I began to see and understand things about myself that I didn't much like, either. Worst of all, I began in that moment, to see a new trackway from my son's beginning to his ending thirty-one years, five months and twenty-six days later. My hands are shaking and painful again. I feel sick. Lovely Donald and I created our son. Perhaps our combined pathologies helped destroy him much more than I had understood up to this precise minute, now. There is always a lot of guilt around when someone takes their own life. Sometimes that guilt has been earned.

I need to stop, breathe, loosen the tension in my hands, in my chest. Breathing in, breathing out. Continue.

It depends, too, what you mean by titanic. In the scale of human history and current world events, my life is just one more life. This is all trivial, of interest only to me and those close to me. Today is 10 June 2018. I watched the TV news earlier, with the main story being the rescue of the twelve young boys and their football coach from a flooded cave system in Thailand. Now that really is a titanic story – of survival, of heroism. It will make a great film. Those boys are at the beginning of their lives too. Who knows what they may go on to achieve? I am much closer to the end of my life, and very unlikely to achieve much at all now. Why bother trying to subdue my shaking hands to the pen and the keyboard? I feel an urgency, a need to communicate my experience, a pressure to continue. I can almost hear a voice saying, '*Keep writing*', and it feels at times as if I am taking dictation – the words seem to come fully formed into my mind. I trust within myself that there is some reason for this. It may be just therapy for me – and that's fine. It may be that I have something to communicate that might be of interest or use to someone else. That's fine too. So I have to keep writing, but you are free to stop reading any time you like. I won't mind.

I'd like to think, though, that at least one person has followed me thus far, and will stay with me to the end. If you are that person, maybe you can explain something to me. In fact, as we go along, I might throw in a few questions – there is much I find incomprehensible. Sometimes, when talking to Lovely Donald and Friend Dick, I felt like a person might feel if they only speak German, and are trying to communicate with someone who only understands Greek. Or even more difficult, if they are trying to communicate with ET, the alien who has just landed on our planet and with whom we share no common frame of reference.

Lying, they both said, is what you have to do if you are going to have affairs. You have to lie to your wife, who might otherwise leave you, and you have to lie to the other woman so that she will continue to fuck you and say she loves you. That's the game, they both said. I suppose I've never been any good at games.

Their bland and blank-faced explanations of the need for lies and the telling of lies left me – where? *Buffering* is the word that seems to fit. Strangely, it left me feeling some slight sympathy with Linda (by this time aka 'The Fuckbitch'). She and I shared the experience of being deceived, inhabited the same planet in the same universe. My husband and Dick came from a planet that orbited a different kind of star in a different kind of universe, governed by a different kind of physics, and different laws of language and meaning.

If, Dear Reader (assuming you exist), you understand Lovely Donald's universe and can explain it to me, I would be very, very grateful. Otherwise... buffering... But I have to finish this download eventually, switch myself off and on again, and get on with life.

'She must have known something...'

Well, of course I knew *something*. The trouble is that you don't always know what it is that you know until you realise, usually too late, what it all means. What you know, after all, is filtered through your beliefs about yourself, other people and the world. My little warning bells tinkled regularly and sometimes quite loudly, but they could always be explained away or dismissed. Lovely Donald was good, very good, at providing plausible explanations for my warning bells, which often left me feeling slightly guilty for having doubted him. And then there was that childlike quality that I mentioned before. I always saw in my mind's eye the baby in the nursery with no consistent carer, no secure attachment. I saw, too, the eleven-year-old at his father's funeral, having his own moment when his life as he knew it to be disappeared, and he learned that he was, in fact, adopted. *'You look so much like your father. It's uncanny, really, given that there is no blood relationship between you, given that you were adopted...'* No harm was intended. That doesn't mean that harm didn't happen. I made allowances. Another insistent image. I have a habit of singing as I go about daily tasks – hoovering, washing up to the sound of 'Onward, Christian soldiers' or 'Scarborough Fair'. I have no musical ability and I can't carry a tune, but I can sing. We can all sing, even if the noise we produce isn't one that anyone else wants to listen to. So I sing. Hymns, old songs, ballads I learned at school fifty-five years ago. It's a habit. I've always done it. I suddenly see myself singing, la-la-ing very loudly, for the last thirty-four years, the singing in my head blocking off doubt.

I had a version of our lives in my head – imperfect, like everyone else's life. I felt uncared-for, unconsidered, in my marriage – would raise this with Lovely Donald, and would be persuaded that he was doing his best, given his personality, early life, commitment to work and general outlook. I remember saying to him that he was always looking outwards, never inwards to home, marriage, family. He used to agree.

But – and Lovely Donald always said that as soon as you say 'but…', you negate everything you've already said – *but* we had the shared task of supporting our son, who needed a lot of support over his life. We had a home, we had our dogs, we had, I thought, some shared interests. Most importantly, I thought, we had shared values. I think I've said that before, but it is important. I believed that ministry was of central importance in Lovely Donald's life, and another broken marriage might jeopardise that for him. I didn't want to do that to him. Let me stress – I was not miserable. There was much in my life to enjoy and I am good – it's not much to claim – at making the best of things, finding what is positive within my day-to-day experience. I was comforted by the good I perceived Donald to be doing in the world.

I used to wish that Lovely Donald communicated more, was more open about his feelings and less dismissive of mine – but it never, even for a second, occurred to me that he was actively deceiving me, our family and everyone around us. It never for a second occurred to me that he was betraying the commitment he had made to the church and the senior clerics who had given him a second chance. I suspected that he had no deep affection for me, that he stayed with me from habit, the desire to protect his ministry and the knowledge that we could better support his children and our son as a couple, but I did believe he felt for me the affection that he was capable of feeling. I never suspected the existence of the visits to brothels or the adventures with the various Lindas. It was not within my world view, my sense of the possible. It never occurred to me. I believed the image of the mostly good, ethically aware clergyman, therapist and all-round caring person. It never occurred to me that Lovely Donald was capable of such deceit over so many years and with so little guilt. As he described his enjoyment of the deception, of getting away with it (maybe even more enjoyable than the sex?), I felt numb. The atmosphere of his planet was too thin, almost toxic. I could not get my breath. I felt too numb, most of the time, for anger. Buffering… Not all the time, though. There was anger.

There used to be a saying: *It is the cobbler's children who have holes in their shoes*. The caring professions make heavy emotional demands on the members of those professions.

There isn't always too much left for the people closest to you, as Lovely Donald used to say. Especially, I suppose, when you are busy having sex with prostitutes and building emotional and physical bonds with a series of Lindas.

Would I have stayed if I had known about the Lindas? I don't know. I doubt it. I'm not sure. It would have depended on the circumstances at the time. Would I have stayed had I known of Lovely Donald's capacity for sustained deceit and his enjoyment of deception? Would I have stayed if I had recognised that he and I came not from different planets but from different universes? Not for a moment. So is it the deceit, the duration of that deceit and his enjoyment of that deceit that makes me numb with shock and a kind of grief, much more than the actual sexual betrayal? Of course. Sex is just sex. The real betrayal – of me, our family, our friends, his congregation, the church and every code of professional ethics he professed to believe in – lies in the pretence, the hypocrisy over years. The absence of guilt or remorse, showing one face to the world, inviting people to trust that face – and giving no clue that that face was just a mask, hiding something far less caring. These are the rocks on which I could be shipwrecked if I don't steer a wise course.

I am not innocent. As I sang away, ignoring all the warning bells (and they did boom as well as tinkle, occasionally), I imposed my version of our life on my experience. I remember troubling dreams, uneasy feelings that things were not as they should be, that I was doing all the compromising in my marriage, to the point of being compromised, not living my own truth. But this is hindsight, again, making sense of feelings after the event that at the time were vague and even guilt-inducing. After all, Donald was such a lovely man in so many ways. Everyone said so. My conscious concerns, such as they were, centred round the balance of power and compromise in my marriage. It never crossed my mind for a single second that Donald, with all his talk of integrity and respect, was capable of the kind of deceit he was practising upon us all. It was not within my mental frame of reference. Wilful blindness? Perhaps. I was not suspicious. Is it possible that my inability, or refusal, to be suspicious, to see what was there to be seen had I looked, enabled Lovely Donald to lead his double (treble? quadruple?) life? It's possible, too, that other people, because they trusted me, ignored any little warning bells of their own because I trusted Donald. One of my nieces said that she had always felt a little uncomfortable around Lovely Donald, 'but everybody seemed to think he was a kind of saint so I thought it was just me.' A friend said something similar. As I've said before, maybe Donald could only be Donald because I am me. The clowns' act is carefully choreographed; and in the 'Lovely Donald and Hoodwinked Hattie' show, timing was everything. I could have asked more questions. I could have made more demands. I could have had a greater sense of self-worth. I hear my family saying loudly, that Lovely Donald was determined to deceive everyone. That's his responsibility, not yours, they say. Indeed so. But I could have asked more questions. An acquaintance, when talking of her own life with a duplicitous man, mentioned feeling like she developed a kind of Stockholm

Syndrome, failed to see how abnormal her life had actually become over time. Snap.

As I write, though, it occurs to me, too, to wonder whether, in claiming a kind of collusion with Lovely Donald, claiming a share of the responsibility for what my son would undoubtedly have called 'this clusterfuck', I am 'bigging myself up', perhaps refusing to accept my own unimportance, my own powerlessness. Nobody likes to feel that they have been deceived and used, after all. I do not like reaching the end of a thirty-four-year marriage and finding out that I was nothing to my husband other than a cover story. Maybe seeing myself as caught in some kind of pathological symbiosis is more palatable than seeing myself as a victim, as someone who was conned by a skilled and clever conman? Having thought of myself, all my life, as an intelligent woman with some insight into human nature, maybe it is just too demeaning to see myself as a victim, a dupe. But, if this isn't too much of a cop-out, it is possible that the truth lies somewhere in between victimhood and co-dependency, somewhere more muddled – the 'debatable land' where the dragons might be hiding.

What do you think?

Yet another insistent image. Have you ever seen the kind of trick photography where the camera focuses in extreme close-up on a very tiny detail of an image or object? As you look, you have no idea what is being shown. Then, as the camera pans away, you see more and more of the image, and eventually there comes a tipping point, and you can see what it is. But even then, you will only recognise what it is if you have a mental frame of reference for that image or object. You have to be able to recognise the type of image or object it is, fit it into your categories of known things. Otherwise it may seem just a meaningless jumble of light and shade.

When Deacon Brodie was finally caught, the good citizens of Edinburgh hanged him. I have often wondered whether he was hanged as much for his ability to deceive people into thinking he was an upright citizen as for his crimes. It bears repeating that nobody likes to be duped.

So, if you are thinking, *She must have known something*, I agree. I must. Sadly, though, I lacked the frame of reference to recognise what it was that I knew. Buffering…

–13–

HELP!

You may remember that I am lost in the heat and humidity of an unknown jungle in an unknown country, quite alone. There are no paths, no landmarks by which I might find my way. I am at the end. I cannot struggle any more. I want my child, who is dead. I could abandon myself to despair now, and let the leeches suck my blood until I am too weak to go on. I'm close to that now. I don't think I've mentioned that I have a progressive neurodegenerative illness that means I respond badly to heat and high humidity. All my symptoms worsen and I become drained and exhausted easily. The jungle is, for me, the worst possible environment. The leeches won't have to work too hard. I am already weakened. Maybe some venomous snake or poisonous spider will come along and show mercy by stinging me and giving me a quick, if painful, end. Perhaps I deserve pain. I could just lie down on the ground now and close my eyes…

Behind my closed eyes I see myself leaving this tired old

body behind, finding my son, having another conversation about Thomas Hobbes or the meaning of life… But my son is dead. And if I don't get up and move, I will be dead too. I do not know whether I will, at the point of death, be reunited with my child. Somehow I doubt it. Nevertheless, it would be so easy just to stay here… give up… I hear an old song in my head – 'I am weary, and sick of trying…' The song continues… 'tired of living, scared of dying…' I am tired of living. I'm not scared of dying. I feel myself fading, fading. Then a thought comes.

If I stay here, nobody will ever know what happened to me. I disappeared one day and never came back. The only clue to where I might have gone was the book lying open on the table by my bed – 'SAS Jungle Survival'. Nothing else. I'm tempted to think that nobody would care deeply or try too hard to find me. I'm a burden and they'd all be better off if I was out of the way, however that came about. Nobody would miss me. They would remember me as the joke, the woman who lived for thirty-four years with a man who constantly and consistently made a fool of her. *What was wrong with her?* they say. *She must have driven Lovely Donald to do what he did. Her son killed himself, you know. She must be pretty toxic…*

I'm not sure that's true, though. Any of it. Thoughts are just thoughts, not facts. It's possible – likely – that people might worry and fret, feel a need to know what happened to me. Maybe it is a cruel thing to do, just to lie here and drown in my own misery, leaving people to wonder what happened, what they did wrong, why I didn't tell them where I was going. If I am going to lie down and die, this is not the way to do it or the place to do it. Nobody was laughing. Everyone grieves for my son in their own individual ways, and now for me too. I examine the evidence. Everyone close to me has been supportive in whatever way they can be. I have been given care, consideration, help – love, even – by many people. Friends, family, my son's friends, strangers... Look at the evidence. I hear the voices of all these people, cheering me on.

I need help. Since this is all happening inside my head, I can bring the help I need. I have a momentary image of men in wetsuits arriving with a stretcher and leech removers and a cool vest... but that's a fantasy, inspired, no doubt, by the Thai cave rescue. There are no rescuers. If I can make my way to a village or find other people somehow, I'm sure they will help me. But first I have to help myself. To start with, I need to stand up. I know how to remove leeches safely. I may not want to do it, but I do know how.

Using the materials to hand – large leaves, vines, bark – I manage to fashion some crude leggings for myself, and wrap my feet in greenness. It's not great, but it is some protection. I walk.

I haven't walked far – maybe 250 yards – when I hear a new sound. Running water? No, that's not it. I listen. I don't believe I'm hearing what I think I'm hearing. I walk another few yards. Suddenly I am out of the jungle. Ahead of me – a road! It's hardly the M6, but there are vehicles – cars, motorbikes, Land Rovers. What looks like it might be a police car is coming towards me. It slows, stops. A woman in uniform gets out. Does she speak English? She does. She has been looking for me. My family reported me missing. She is taking me to the nearby hospital for a bath, a change of clothes, some food. They will disinfect and dress my various injuries to protect me against infection. They will contact my family. I will go home.

I am still weary and sick of trying. I still feel I can't do this any more. I still want my child, who isn't coming back. My bones hurt.

We live in impermanence. All things are passing. This will pass. Lovely Donald is dead. There are many questions that will never have answers. I am alive, though, and there are people who care about me. I do not have to hide. I only have one face – I left the clown masks at the circus – so my life is much easier than Lovely Donald's can have been, for all his bluster about enjoying deceit. I grieve for my son. I grieve for his life and his death and for his inability to see that the meaning of life is life. I would like to send him a postcard – *Wish you were here*. I will always grieve for my son until I take my final breath. The grief stays the same. But life grows around the grief, if I allow myself to participate in life in my own small, tired way.

I think I am beginning to understand the dragons now. My son collected dragons, and when I redecorated Lovely Donald's room, I brought my son's dragons out of the loft. I dusted them and put them on display in the new room. It needed light, air and dragon energy. I feel more and more certain that I am a dragon whisperer.

– 14 –

WHY DIDN'T I NOTICE? LIFE GETS IN THE WAY

What distracted me? Occupied my mind and my energy enough that I failed to focus on the wasteland that my marriage had become (or maybe always was)? All I can say is that life got in the way, as it does.

My son always needed a lot of support, a lot of time, a lot of energy. And, because of my own health, energy was in short supply.

My health meant that life increasingly became a struggle for me. I was often exhausted and severe attacks of vertigo proved debilitating and disabling. Lovely Donald never quite seemed to believe that I was ill – surely I could be better if I tried harder? Thought more positively? As I battled on through various unproductive diagnoses and the many compromises forced upon me by my often weird symptoms, I wasn't sure how much harder I could try, how much more positive it was possible to be. When a new, young, enthusiastic consultant finally sent me for the right tests and facilitated a correct diagnosis, it was a relief. Even though it was a scary diagnosis – there was no cure and not much in the way of treatment and the illness is progressive – at least I had an explanation for all my years of troublesome symptoms.

I realise, with hindsight, how much I went through this process alone. Lovely Donald only ever accompanied me to my various medical appointments when the appointment letter told me that I needed to be accompanied, usually because the tests might leave me unable to drive. I realise, too, how much he used my necessary absences to facilitate his relationship with his Lollipop Lady, which was then at its height – this was all happening before Poor Hubby, Linda's husband, walked in on them.

Work was also an issue. Although I was rarely absent from work for health reasons, medical advice dictated that I give up my full-time and very demanding job as a social work manager at the age of forty-six. I was beyond belief fortunate in receiving a pension, but after a couple of years, I began to do bits and pieces of part-time work. This and that. Here and there. I learned new skills and used them, partly for money and partly for my own interest and self-respect. Lovely Donald was supportive of my desire to return to at least some work. That felt helpful at the time, but I wonder now what his motivation might have been. The work I did meant that I was regularly and predictably out of the house for hours at a time.

And let's not forget the church. Although not really a Christian, let alone an Anglican, I did want to support Lovely

Donald's ministry because he presented it as being central to his life and identity. He certainly seemed to be doing a good job, if you forget about the admin. At first I involved myself in the life of the church in the way that clergy spouses are able to do, and I enjoyed much of it. I liked the people and I liked the sense of community, and I did feel that I had something useful to offer. As time went by, though, I began to feel increasingly unwelcome. Lovely Donald, it seemed, did not really appreciate my involvement beyond the cleaning rota and occasional special events. I began to feel that maybe I was, in a sense and certainly not deliberately, 'muscling in' on his territory. I couldn't possibly understand the life of the church, he told me, because I lacked an Anglican background. Fair enough, I felt – and I had reached a point where I needed to simplify my life anyway. This was all happening before my eventual diagnosis, and at a point where I knew I had to let go of something. I didn't want to give up my job, so I gave up most of my involvement with the church. Lovely Donald appeared to welcome, even encourage, my withdrawal, which confirmed me in continuing to withdraw. Maybe there was a little bit of 'I won't push myself in where I'm not wanted' childishness on my part too?

Lovely Donald, throughout all the years I knew him, was massively and chaotically untidy. He never offered much day-to-day practical help in the house – on the plea of being too busy (all those trips to Yorkshire probably didn't help). He would say that my standards were too high – trust me, he is the only person ever to think so! I'm fairly untidy myself, but I do have limits. He would say that I would only complain that he didn't do the job properly, whatever it was. But – what would you have done? Have said? If, for example, he did hoover the carpet, he would hoover the bits that showed up to a point, but would lose interest halfway through and wander off, leaving the task unfinished and the hoover where someone would trip over it. I reached a point of saying that if I asked him to do something and he wasn't going to do it, he should just refuse. At least that way I'd know where I stood. As it was, I would ask him to wash the pots, say, and rely on his promise to do it. Then I'd come back, often unwell, and find I'd have to do it myself. Maybe I overreacted? Maybe I should never have asked him to do anything? But he lived in the house too and I rarely asked him to do very much. His argument was always that he worked many more hours than I did and had to be out of the house much more frequently. I made allowances. I also didn't often have the energy to argue – though I did manage it sometimes. I used to wonder why he would watch me struggle with something and never offer to help. I felt uncared-for. I'd voice this – not angrily, but as a problem that we needed to try to address. As always, Donald would say he was doing his best. And perhaps he was.

Lovely Donald never wanted to 'waste time' on routine maintenance of the house – painting a wall, fixing a plug, tidying the garden. My life became one long cost/benefit analysis. Can I do this myself? Can I pay someone to do it for me? Can I bribe or cajole my son to help? Does it really matter if it doesn't get done at all? Is the achievement of this task worth the energy expended to get it done? When the Diocesan Property Manager made his quinquennial inspection of the vicarage, he would comment on the mould on the grouting on the shower (my fault) but not on the messiness of Lovely Donald's cobweb-festooned office that he never cleaned or allowed me to clean. At times this felt like a male conspiracy and then I would rebuke myself for being paranoid. Are you thinking that maybe I wasn't paranoid at all? Or, as the poster on my office wall once said, JUST BECAUSE YOU'RE PARANOID, IT DOESN'T MEAN THEY'RE NOT OUT TO GET YOU?

And all this practical life at home was taking place against the background of wider family concerns and traumas. My son, over the years, had various kinds of involvement with adolescent and adult mental health services. He was, at times, offered some help, but somehow it was never really the right kind of help. He and I spent quite a lot of effort and energy trying to work out what kind of help might be helpful, but without much success. Things would go well for a while, but then old problems would surface or new ones develop. I sometimes felt that I was on the edge of anxiety all the time. I felt a failure as a parent – and in many ways I probably was a failure as a parent. Lovely Donald was always fairly dismissive of my concerns and of our son's. To be fair, he did, I know, worry about our son, but didn't have the patience to engage with him, talk to him, take him seriously. Donald would cite how busy he was with his two jobs and his counselling work, how tiring it all was. And his own health wasn't good, largely the result of his destructive relationship with food and alcohol, but also in part because of working nights over many years. I did my best to prepare healthy food, to 'keep the show on the road'. I thought I was doing the right thing for everyone. I never focused on the gap between what I thought and how I felt. I trusted my rational mind.

If you are wondering about a similar gap in your own life, wonder a bit more, examine that gap, interrogate it. Above all, don't ignore it. I think now that I used my rational mind and what seemed to be the evidence all around me to suppress the promptings of my gut instinct, my intuition. Hindsight again, I know.

There was other stuff too. Lovely Donald was engaged with tracing firstly his birth mother, and then learning about his birth father, who had died years earlier. Donald did manage to meet members of his father's family, both in England and in Poland. It was an emotional journey.

Over the years, Donald had talked much about the 'primal wound' of adoption, and the feelings of rejection he experienced around his adoption. I helped him to trace his birth mother, and that was a relatively straightforward process. He was able to meet her and her husband and his two half-siblings, and form some kind of a bond with them. His imperative, though, was always to trace his birth father, and this proved to be a longer and much more difficult journey. Eventually, after years of trying, he learned that his birth father had died long before Donald's search began, leaving behind him a complex history of family breakdown and fractured relationships. Donald was able to have some limited contact with those paternal half-siblings who were prepared to have contact with him, and through one of them, he was able to trace his father's family in Poland. His uncle was still alive, though in his late eighties, and if Donald wanted to meet him, it was best not to waste time. He was able to travel to Poland, meet his uncle and cousins, and learn about his father's early life. I'd hoped he would find what he needed, some resolution, through all this. He was reluctant to discuss any of this with anyone and seemed to bury it in some rarely examined corner of his psyche.

After Donald died, it took me many months to sort out the paper mountain he left behind him, jumbled up in no particular order, all having to be sorted through. Important financial information might be stuck inside a pile of old takeaway menus, no system to any of it. I found it very poignant to discover that in all the muddle and confusion of his life, there was a single beautifully kept and organised file, paperwork completely in order, preserved in plastic wallets, neat and pristine. This was the file that contained the information about his adoption and his search for his birth parents, and records and photos of all the contacts he had been able to have with both sides of his family of origin. It seemed to have been hidden away. It had certainly never been shared with me or with his sons, whose heritage it was. Perhaps some wounds run too deep to be allowed the light of day. I gave this file to my stepson.

Alongside all this, my mother had her own continuing and serious health problems, which were always a concern. My father met a sudden death at the hands of a careless driver who was in a hurry. I will leave you to imagine the aftermath of that.

Some years before this, my youngest sister had encountered her own careless driver in a hurry – a very young man driving a very fast car. He fractured her skull and fractured her leg – a complex and dangerous set of injuries. Although she had always been smaller, slower and more frail than the rest of us, she was ostensibly a young and healthy woman. It was her inability to recover from these injuries as well as her doctors expected that led to her eventual diagnosis of mitochondrial disease. Her problems increased over time, and she never fully recovered from the trauma of her injuries and the later trauma of our father's death. It was the complexities of mitochondrial disease following a bad fall and another fractured femur that led to her own eventual death at the age of forty, four years later, after a truly horrendous six weeks of suffering – for her, and so for all of us.

Lovely Donald was sometimes *missing in action* over these years. He didn't seem able to offer me much in the way of emotional support or practical assistance, but I muddled through. The dark humour my son and I shared did help. I kept calm(ish) and carried on.

Of all the revelations of the last year, the thing I have found most deeply hurtful and distressing and incomprehensible was learning that Donald may have used my necessary absences when my sister was in hospital as opportunities to visit Lollipop Linda. As I – the driver in my family – took my mother, my huggy sister and myself to the specialist unit where my sick sister lay, sometimes driving more than 400 miles in a day, Lovely Donald was 'too busy' to remember to buy bread and milk and keep food in the fridge. He still had to work, he said, and sort out our son's lifts as Mum's taxi and adequate public transport were equally unavailable AND he had to walk the dog we had at the time. As well as all this, he had to contend with the demands of his role as a clergyman and his paid work as a night-duty social worker – it was almost impossible for him to 'keep all his plates spinning'. He was 'meeting himself coming back'. Of course he was. He was meeting himself coming back from his 100-mile round trip to fuck the Lollipop Lady. (Am I displaying a bit of rage here? I certainly feel it in this moment.)

He hadn't managed to find the time to make sure that there was food in the house for me to eat when I arrived home at 5 a.m. one day, after a round trip of almost 500 miles to discuss my sick sister's dire prognosis with the specialists in charge of her care. It was a distressing day. And then on the way home we got stuck for hours in a long, snow-filled delay on the motorway. Teeth-gritted Determination helped me take my mother and huggy sister home and then get home myself.

Lovely Donald was out – working? – when I finally arrived back at my house. My son heard me come in, got up, made me coffee – fortunately we both took our coffee black. We drove the three and a half miles to the nearest twenty-four-hour supermarket, where we bought croissants and bacon. We shared these with Lovely Donald when he arrived home shortly after we got back, and just as the bacon was sizzling. He'd had a hideously busy night, he said, in his job as a night-duty social worker. He was almost as exhausted as I was. I sympathised. I wonder now if he'd had a rough journey back from Yorkshire, given the unexpected snow? But I can never know the truth of it.

I wonder, too, if he ever considered that all this deception might be a bad idea. A moment's thought might have told him this, after all. But, as somebody or other once said, a moment is a long time and thought is a painful process.

As I write down my recollections of these events, I remember my friend's comment about her own life with a serial adulterer (albeit one not quite so skilled at deceit). Do you remember I told you earlier about how she had talked about feeling as if she developed a kind of Stockholm syndrome, failing to realise how abnormal her life had become? Of course I can see the clues to Lovely Donald's duplicity now, looking backwards. At the time, I suppose I was too immersed in the busyness and stress of my life to have the time and space and energy to really listen to all those little warning bells I kept right on hearing or to consider what they might mean. Life got in the way.

And there were other considerations too. I was busy and tired and tired and busy. Like Lovely Donald, I had worked as a night-duty social worker and I knew how punishingly busy the work could be. It gave an explanation for his absences and unavailability. I had questioned Lovely Donald's wisdom in taking on his role as a parish priest in addition to his paid job and other commitments, but accepted his insistence that he had a vocation, a calling. I was still tired and busy and busy and tired. Everyone knew that Lovely Donald was a good and caring man – they told me so repeatedly and the evidence was there in the queue of people thanking him. I stifled doubt. It's possible that I lost connectedness to myself in all this busyness. In losing connectedness to myself, I also lost connectedness to the world around me and so became easier to deceive. It's a theory.

Writing now about what I want to call all this shite – defiantly, as Lovely Donald hated swearing except when he did it himself – all this writing is a way of putting some distance between myself and the experience, standing back from it so that I am not overwhelmed and destroyed by it. My mind snags on the thought that Lovely, Lovely Donald could use my sick sister's dying as an opportunity to visit a woman he met on a dating site for adulterers. How could he do this? God knows – but she isn't telling.

So I do what I need to do in order not to lose myself in the unreal and perilous landscape of my life with Lovely Donald. I see myself mired in quicksand, being dragged down into mud and destruction. So I remind myself that it's over, after all, that life. I have a different life now. I continue to find my way through, carefully, cautiously, step by step by step. I could still face shipwreck or be lost in the quicksand. It isn't always easy to distinguish between the life-saving beams of the lighthouse and the false lights shown by wreckers. It's huge, that realisation that half my life and all of my son's life have been lived in an unreal world of deceit and unconcern. How do I live with that?

Well, I either live with it – or I die. Can you think of a third choice? So I live.

– 15 –

'THERE'S NO SMOKE
WITHOUT FIRE...' (2)

There's an old song that keeps pushing itself into my mind. I can't remember the title, the singer or most of the words, but the same couple of phrases have become an earworm in my brain. It's something about circles and spirals and windmills in the mind – maybe you know the song?

My thoughts about whether I should/shouldn't, can/can't write about my son revolve endlessly round my head, like windmill sails in a gale, rattling and banging. I lost patience with telling his story as a tale of knights and maidens and dragons – and if I lost patience with it, I guess you, the reader, might lose patience too. But I'm not sure and I dither. But if I am going to tell it at all, I need to get on with it. So, having decided to tell Murf's story, I've decided to tell it as follows. (I think. I might change my mind...)

It's almost two years now since I began writing this book. You might reasonably think that I began at page one and worked my way, page by page, to where we are now. That's not quite what happened, though. I wrote and revised and rewrote, and the chapters came as they came, which was not necessarily in the order in which they appear here in the weird book. Had I reframed these events as fiction, I could have made them flow more logically, but that's not how it was. I've floated here and there in time and space, landing in versions of reality and then moving on to some other part of the multiverse.

Beyond acknowledging his death and my own grief, I spoke little of my son in the first four drafts of the book. People have asked me if Murf's death was too raw and painful to speak of then. It will always be raw and painful – what else could it be? – but I don't think that was the reason I didn't say much about him. I began writing less than eight weeks after my husband died, and I was angry. I felt, then, that my husband did not deserve to be in the same book as my son; that my son, basically a decent man, was too good to share space with his father. (Note that I was thinking then of 'my' son rather than 'our' son.) That anger has subsided now. Although perhaps natural in the circumstances, it was pointless and could harm only me. I chose not to feed the anger and it has faded away, at least most of the time. After all, whatever else happened, my husband was and remains my son's father. That's a fact. Therefore they are in the same book whether I like it or not.

There have been other, more compelling considerations in deciding whether or not to talk in greater detail about my son. I am very aware that his story is lengthy and complex and raises many contentious issues about our legal system and the role of the mental health services. Can I do justice to the complexity of all this in the context of my weird book?

The mental health services have felt the impact of the austerity agenda. Murf, at a time of great need, received a less-than-adequate response from those services – no fault of individual clinicians but a reflection of the difficulties they face as our health service comes under increasing pressure. The more I think about this, the more I wonder whether Murf needs a book all to himself. It is a big story and bears a more detailed telling than is possible here. And that consideration remains. As I have begun to write about Murf and about what happened to him in the last fifteen months of his life, and about the impact of all that on his father and on me, I have realised more and more that somebody should write a book about it. A whole book.

Even more compelling, for me, is the question I ask myself constantly – would Murf want to be in my book? And I can't ask him, can I? And I don't know. He might. He might not. If he could read the book and thought it was drivel, he definitely wouldn't want to be in it; if he thought it was pretty good, then he'd probably claim his place. But if he were here to read it, I probably wouldn't be writing it. More circles and spirals. And the windmill sails go clattering round…

Murf was both very open, often, for example, telling me much more about his love life than I really wanted to know, but also very private, very careful about what he chose to share with the wider world. Although he used social media, he did not live his life there and certainly felt that some things are private. Is it right to talk about his life when he cannot give permission? Clatter, clatter...

It is impossible to tell the story of Murf's last fifteen months without talking about one other person. This other person – in the dragons and knights version of this story she appears as the Lady Natalya of the Land of Desolation – made false allegations of domestic violence against Murf, which took the seven longest months of our lives to untangle. She was subsequently discredited and proved herself a liar in the Family Court, but this did not diminish the impact of the wrecking ball she sent hurtling into all our lives. The magistrates in the Family Court, in their written judgement, completely vindicated Murf and stated that they believed that Lady Natalya was motivated by a malicious desire to cause problems for him in his work. Murf's subsequent complaint about the actions of the police was upheld by the police professional standards body – but Natalya was, at least to begin with, a skilled and clever liar.

And whenever I have to tell this story, I always feel compelled to add that I can prove what I am saying. There's always a sense, real or imagined, that people are thinking, *Well, she would say that, wouldn't she? And we all know that there's no smoke without fire...* But I **can** prove what I am saying. Feel free to come along and check my paperwork (mine now that Murf is no longer here), if you feel so inclined. That tension, though, that anxiety that other people will react with cynicism and disbelief to Murf's story, reflects his experience in the seven months of his ordeal, and then in the remaining eight months of his life, as I witnessed (and experienced myself on occasion).

After all, everyone knows that there is no smoke without fire.

His decision to end his life was his own. From adolescence onwards he had struggled with life and with the seductiveness of death, and had taken an overdose at the age of seventeen. He had almost immediately sought help, and appeared, back then, to have chosen life – but, although there were no more suicide attempts until close to the end, that choice was always ambivalent, never wholehearted. Murf always struggled with life, and it took courage for him to stay in this world as long as he did. Many factors played into that final moment when, all alone, he chose to leave. It's likely that it was, in the end, an impulsive choice, born of a perfect storm of circumstances that came together at a particular time. It might have been different on a different day, or if the events of those last few days had been changed ever so slightly. It would certainly have been different if Murf had remembered that 'suicide doesn't end the pain – it just passes it on to someone else'.

I attach no blame to anyone – Murf made his own choice – but suicide inevitably creates guilt and questioning in those people who are close to the person who has died. There is a last straw, or a collection of last straws that bring about the ending on a particular day at a particular time.

One of Murf's last straws was a chance encounter in a bar with a former colleague. After the final court hearing, Murf had begun to pick up his paused and injured life once again, and a part of this was his attempt to resume some kind of social life. So there he is, in a bar, all tentative in his attempts to find a way to be. There he saw an ex-colleague, someone with whom he'd got along, not a close friend. Let's call him Dave. 'Hello, Dave,' said Murf. 'Long time, no see. Can I buy you a pint?'

Speaking as much to the people around as to Murf, Dave's reply was, 'Fuck off, Murf. I don't take drinks from men who hit women.' This was a perfectly reasonable response on Dave's part, wasn't it? After all, he'd heard the rumours and the stories and he, like you and like me, knew that there is no smoke without fire…

I wasn't there, of course. Murf was crushed by this encounter when he told me about it later. Natalya's allegations, false though they might have been, would always follow him, he said, always undermine him, always colour other people's views. No smoke without fire – such a cruel phrase. Do you see why it rouses such fury in me? If you find yourself tempted to use the phrase in the future, please remember Murf, and think again.

I said the usual things about people having short memories, about today's gossip being forgotten tomorrow as people move on to the next bit of drama about other people's lives. *Just give it a year*, I said. *Why not make the court judgement public*, I said. *Let the truth circulate, as well as the lies.*

But despite everything, and despite advice from friends, family, colleagues, the lawyers involved and even the magistrates, Murf was and remained quite protective of the Lady Natalya of the Land of Desolation. (Of course that is not her real name but I feel that it suits her.) He flatly refused to share the written court judgement beyond a very small number of people – close family, a couple of friends and his employer, who had to see it in order to be able to reinstate him at work.

He worked with very vulnerable people and thus was subject to enhanced police checks, and had been suspended from work – an important part of his identity and support network – for the whole seven months it took for this sorry process to reach its conclusion. He said that the Lady Natalya had done what she had done because she was damaged and mentally fragile. 'She has enough problems to deal with without me showing her up in public,' he said. 'I'd just be looking for revenge if I did that, and that would only diminish me. It wouldn't change anything.' And he stuck to that until he died, despite the problems it caused him. (Don't forget that there is no smoke without fire… Of course it caused him problems. Remember Dave? He wasn't alone in his comments.)

After Murf's death, I gave Murf's friends permission to share that court judgement with anyone who might be interested. I wanted him to be publicly vindicated in death as he had refused to be in life. I also shared the fact that the complaint that Murf's solicitor had chivvied him into making against the police had been upheld. Did I do the right thing? I don't know. I did what I did. When I thought about all that had happened and the role Lady Natalya had played, I used to imagine her cold, dead body lying on the cold tiles of my kitchen floor. It didn't help. Appealing as the image was at the time, it's gone now. I remember Murf's thoughts on the futility of revenge, and his desire to be a better person, to accept the judgement as vindication enough by itself without needing to respond destructively or doing to Natalya what she had tried to do to him. I hope that allowing the court judgement to be circulated was not just an act of revenge, though there might have been an element of the desire for revenge present. My main motivation, though, was the desire to protect my child. It mattered not, really, what I'd said – Murf's friends would have shared the judgement anyway.

And this brings me to yet more windmills clattering in my should I/shouldn't I tell Murf's story. He hadn't wanted the details shared in his lifetime partly because he had wanted to protect the Lady Natalya from the consequences of her actions. I went against his wishes when he was no longer here, so unable to give consent to his story being shared. How far am I bound by his wishes after his death?

Throughout Murf's long academic career, I used to proofread his essays and assignments for him, and we would discuss and debate what he wrote. He would even, very occasionally, take on board some of my comments – which always gave me great satisfaction and some pride. I remember reading and discussing the essay on deathbed-promising that Murf wrote when he was working towards his Master of Research degree in 2013. He would most certainly say that I am not bound by his wishes now he is dead, as this was the view he argued in his essay. But questions remain for me – more noisy, clattering windmills. How do I choose what is the right thing, the ethical thing, to do? In a recent discussion about other, unrelated issues, a friend of Murf's said that if Murf had wanted to influence events now, he should have stuck around to have his twopenn'orth – and that comment, though brutal and heart-piercing, struck me with the force of truth. So here I am, telling Murf's story, in what is for me an unusually straightforward way.

I remember a question Murf asked himself and me, from the moment all this began until the day of his death. He had loved Natalya and, despite all the problems, believed (or wanted to believe) that she loved him. 'What's wrong with me,' he would say, 'that would make her do this to me?' Try as I might, I could never really get him to reframe that question, to ask what might be wrong with her. I've asked myself that same question since I learned the truth about Lovely Donald's secret lives. 'What's wrong with me that made him do this?' I've understood why Murf found it so difficult to reframe the question as I'd suggested; I've struggled to do it myself.

Murf met Natalya through some mutual friends with whom he shared a house. They needed another person in the house share, and so Natalya moved in. She and Murf grew close. He talked to me over time about the pros and cons of becoming involved with a housemate… I listened and encouraged him to make his own choices. Why wasn't I screaming, 'Don't do it!'? There were possibilities and pitfalls in this situation that never occurred to Murf or to me because they were so far outside our experience, values and ideas about the world and other people as to be literally unthinkable. They did not appear on our radar. We never imagined what would happen. Unknown unknowns.

Soon, Murf and Natalya became a couple. Shortly afterwards, the other couple in the house share changed jobs and moved down south. Rather than find someone else to join them in the house, Murf and Natalya moved to a smaller house where they could afford the rent by themselves. It seemed to be a joint decision. I helped them with the move.

At first all seemed well(ish). Early on my husband had some doubts about Natalya, felt there was something untrustworthy about her, though he was unable to identify exactly what his concerns were. I wonder if he recognised something in her that he shared, a willingness and ability to deceive? I had some niggling doubts myself, but Natalya and Murf seemed happy, and we hoped for the best. They were adults, after all. Murf was in his late twenties by this time, and Natalya was a few years older. We made her as welcome as she would allow and continued to hope for the best.

I struggled to get a sense of Natalya's personality. She seemed to shun contact with us, and Murf explained this by saying she'd always had a difficult relationship with her own family and was suspicious of parents. I wanted to like her, and knew of no positive reason to dislike her, but I felt uneasy, though less so than my husband. Murf seemed happy, at least to begin with, and I wanted all to be well. It's so easy, isn't it, to ignore those little warning bells?

Over time, though, they began to chime a little more insistently. I noticed that in the stories told by Natalya about her family, her work colleagues, her friends and the medical and psychiatric professionals involved in her care, she always presented herself as a victim of their bullying or their incompetence. Could this really be true of everyone in her life? Could every family member, every colleague be abusive and bullying? Every single health professional uncaring and incompetent? 'She's had a tough life,' said Murf. 'It's made her a little bit suspicious of other people in general...'

I kept my own counsel. Murf was fiercely protective of his independence and his autonomy, and I wanted to keep the channels of communication open. After all, we can't always like the people our children like, can we? So my husband and I both worked on trying to build some rapport with Natalya and to focus on the strengths, on the fact that she and Murf appeared happy together. We tried to offer support or help where we could, when asked, and we worked to maintain positive relationships with Natalya and Murf as a couple.

And I'm not sure what else we could have done other than what we did, without interfering in what, after all, was not our business. If everything went wrong, I rationalised to myself, at least we'd be able to help Murf pick up the pieces...

All continued to seem well(ish) as Murf and Natalya made a life together, but gradually things changed. Murf had a close circle of friends with whom he always kept in contact and with whom he shared many interests – medieval re-enactment, Dungeons and Dragons, Magic the Gathering, real ale, music, philosophy and the arts. He socialised, went for meals, went clubbing to Goth clubs, went to concerts and gigs and met up with friends to share their nerdish interests. He enjoyed reading Terry Pratchett's books – 'the man has a brain the size of a planet!' – and he collected dragons. All this, like his work, was important to Murf and formed a strong network of support at difficult times. He and a female friend, a PhD candidate, co-authored a chapter for a work of popular philosophy in the Blackwell popular philosophy series – Murf was very happy when he finally held in his hands 'his' book, complete with its dragon on the front cover. He finished his MRes and began a PhD himself, specialising in the philosophy of Thomas Hobbes. I remember well the 7 a.m. telephone conversations with Murf when he used me as a sounding board for his ideas on Hobbes, or chatted, as he used to say, about 'random shit' like politics, Dr Who and the world in general. I miss those conversations. I put his ancient copy of Hobbes's *Leviathan* in his coffin later, together with his own book, some wine gums and a bag of coffee. I didn't want to send him empty-handed on his final journey out of this world.

Murf lived about fifteen miles away from his father and me, so not far. He worked, though, only about a five-minute drive away, and often used to call in on his way to or from work. We saw him, or spoke to him, several times a week most weeks. Very infrequently, we'd meet up with him and Natalya and go for a curry. The little niggling warning bells continued to tinkle. (Why can't these bloody bells just stop tinkling mysteriously and say what they mean?)

Gradually, though, and almost imperceptibly at first, all of us, friends and family, saw less and less of Murf as he withdrew from his normal haunts and pastimes. He and I no longer went to concerts or the theatre together as we had done from time to time for several years (something else I miss. I owe the little I know of Wagner to Murf). He dropped out of his PhD. He continued to work at his job, though, and talked about making a career in social care rather than in academia as he'd originally planned. He was busy at work, and busy driving Natalya to her various medical appointments – she had both physical and mental health issues. Of course he had less time for friends and family… Of course. We reassured ourselves that all was well, but doubts continued to surface.

We all noticed on the increasingly rare occasions when we did see Murf, that he was changing. He looked harried, a bit scruffy, and was irritable and short-tempered. He lost weight he didn't need to lose. He began to refuse new opportunities both at work and in his social and academic life. Friends saw him no longer, and if they did meet him by chance, they felt that he tried to escape from them as quickly as politeness allowed. The interests he'd followed for so long seemed to interest him less.

I know now how concerned his friends were, but learned this only after the bad stuff happened. Murf withdrew from contact with us, too, but we would have been even more worried than we were if we'd known he'd also largely dropped out of his friendship groups.

I know now about the ripples of anxiety and concern that were spreading around Murf at this time, but he resisted all attempts to reach out to him, sometimes angrily. He was changing…

A couple of Murf's friends, who knew the Lady Natalya well, had seen at close quarters some of her interactions with Murf, and had experienced her anger when they called to see Murf or invited him out. They were beginning to talk among themselves about the phrase that was becoming more widely known at that time – 'coercive control'.

A pattern was emerging whereby Natalya was picking quarrels with Murf's friends, closing off their contact with

Murf, isolating him more and more from everything and everyone, like an apex predator isolating a vulnerable animal from the herd before moving in for the kill. Murf's friends understood Murf's vulnerabilities and were afraid that he was being damaged, even destroyed.

In their individual ways they all tried to give Murf the same message: 'She's destroying you and alienating you from all your supports. Get rid – I say this as your friend.'

Murf wasn't listening, or if he was, he wasn't acting on their concerns and was rebuffing all their attempts to keep in touch and offer support.

I look at the page as I write and see my paragraphs becoming shorter and shorter. I want to tell this part of the story quickly, get it over with, give you the facts as I know them. It is hard to relive these weeks and months.

At the time we could still hope that it would all be all right in the end. But I know the end now, and it will never be all right.

Could any of us have done anything differently? Could we have changed the outcome if we'd respected Murf's autonomy less and interfered more?

I remember a dream I had a few years earlier, when Murf had first left home and before he met Natalya. It was a time of hope, when things seemed to be going well for him and his ambitions seemed to be achievable. I wanted to believe that all could be well, or well enough, but my dream was expressing something different. There were no images in this dream. I was in a place of complete darkness, impenetrable blackness all around me. I felt desolate and powerless. Within the dream I begin to see a faint lightening at the edge of the darkness, a faint glow that I know to be a huge fire, a long way away and out of my sight. It is destroying everything. I don't know how I know this, but I do. And then I hear a voice speaking quietly and without emotion. It is the voice of an unknown man saying over and over again, '*Crash and burn, crash and burn, crash and burn.*'

I woke up alone in my bed and wept. I felt overwhelmed, I remember, doom-laden, trapped in helplessness and hopelessness. My waking self knew that this dream was somehow about Murf, but I didn't know how to interpret the dream or what to do about it. These messages that come from deep inside us, from our unconscious self, are often indirect and unclear, impossible to act on because they give no explanations, no advice or clear line to follow. The feeling of that dream never left me and is with me still. I've pondered it in my heart over years. I think I understand it now, but now it is too late.

I find myself, for the moment, unable to continue. Sometimes the sheer physical burden of grief, its weight and its relentlessness bring me to my knees. I need to stop, eat something, throw a ball for my dogs, live in this moment, breathe. I'm not going to leave you dangling. I will tell you the rest of Murf's story. But not right at this moment.

Back soon.

− 16 −

'THERE'S NO SMOKE WITHOUT FIRE...' (3)

It occurs to me that you might need a chronology to help you to navigate your way through this story. But where to begin? Lovely Donald and I moved in together in September 1983, and Murf was born in December 1984. But this is a tale of damage and how damage breeds damage. So should I begin with Lovely Donald's birth in 1947, when he was effectively abandoned at the age of six weeks and spent the next nine months in a residential nursery before being placed for adoption? Or my own childhood? Or Murf's premature birth and traumatic first weeks of life? Or even with Natalya's childhood traumas of serious illness and difficult relationships? Where is the beginning? Let's just keep it simple for now.

Natalya made her allegations in February 2015. The legal processes ground on until the final court hearing in September 2015, when Murf was cleared of all wrongdoing. He returned to work in October 2015, and we hoped all would be well. His boss, seeing him for the first time in six months, said that he looked 'hollowed-out, eviscerated'. I suppose that being trapped in this world of false allegations and disbelief and confusion does scrape away at who you are. I felt it myself.

Murf seemed to be drawing together the threads of his life, finding new ways of being and picking up old interests. It was almost possible to be hopeful – or was it simply that we wanted to be hopeful? Lovely Donald's health, on the decline for some years before this, was worsening, and his refusal to take medical advice put us all under pressure. Murf's comment – 'Dad's even more self-destructive than I am…' I remember feeling exhausted, and I remember how hard it felt to keep on moving through the days, doing what needed to be done, trying to keep the house, the dogs, Lovely Donald all afloat and provide support for Murf… I lost my balance, both literally – it's a symptom of my illness – and metaphorically. I missed the moment when Murf might have been saved. But maybe he had to want to be saved in order to save himself. There was always this ambivalence about life, this flirtation with death.

The end, when it came, came quickly. Murf seemed to be struggling, but coping. Therapy was discussed, though Murf was unsure about pursuing it. He was making plans, though, and coping well at work… I hoped I could hope.

Then, for whatever reason, Murf became overwhelmed. He took an overdose, called for help, was treated for the physical effects and seemed to have escaped any long-term physical consequences. He was discharged from hospital without any psychiatric follow-up. He seemed quite positive and was continuing to make plans for the future. His employers were supportive. His friends rallied round. Was he going to choose life?

By this point Murf was sharing a house with friends who had supported and encouraged him through the previous year. When, at 9.16 p.m. on Monday 16 May 2016, my phone rang and I saw his friend's name appear, my first thought was, *I wonder why Murf is using Mike's phone?* But the feeling that accompanied the thought was one of cold dread. When I heard Mike's voice, not Murf's, on the other end of the phone, all I could say was, 'Is he dead?' And he was.

There is much I could write of the six weeks between Murf's death and his funeral, the formalities of death, the dealings with the coroner's office, the visits I made to my son in the mortuary, sometimes with Lovely Donald but mostly alone or with Murf's friends. Then the funeral. Then the idea for his Going Away Party and Final Aerial Transit, the distraction of the planning, and the appropriateness of the occasion – 15 October 2016. Then came the long wait for the inquest, which finally happened on 11 May 2017. More lawyers. Dialogues with the Mental Health Trust. And over it all – Grief. A part of me will forever be sitting in my chair, in my conservatory, listening to the audiobook of *We Are All Completely Beside Ourselves* whilst Lovely Donald is watching TV in the living room. My phone rings – I see Mike's name. I try to think, *Why is Murf using Mike's phone...?* This happens every day.

And where was Lovely Donald in all this? Well, he was grieving, in shock, finding it hard to think or plan. Telling my stepson that he'd fucked up everything all his life. He wanted me to plan, suggest the choices and decisions, give him tasks to do... and that was fine. He was becoming visibly more and more unwell, but reacted with apathy or anger to expressions of concern. He had made it clear, to me and to his doctors, that I should not discuss his health with them. Like Murf, he was an adult with the capacity to make choices... He wanted, he said, to reach the biblical 'threescore years and ten', and he made it to threescore years and ten plus four months.

Fast forward again to 6 October 2017... We had returned from holiday on 30 September, and Donald's worsening condition was becoming increasingly obvious. By 6 October, he was too ill to argue or to walk away, and so I 'kidnapped' him and sought medical help. You know what happened after that – his admission to hospital, the Shattering and all that followed, and, eventually, Donald's death on 4 February 2018.

'And I only am escaped alone to tell thee...'

I began to write. I like to read detective stories and murder mysteries, in much the same way as I like crossword puzzles. They often have neat endings. Something I read just a couple of days ago in Andrew Taylor's book, *The Mortal Sickness* made me smile in a kind of recognition: *'Perhaps this was why she needed to write; it gave her the illusion that it was possible to tidy up experience.'*

But the way I have written this book shows that experience rejects tidying up. You and I are untethered here. So what has sustained me through my life in the last few years is kindness. There's a poem I've always loved since I first encountered it a few years ago, but I have read it almost daily since Murf died, and it helps me to navigate the days.

> *'Before you know what kindness really is
> you must lose things...'*
>
> **Naomi Shihab Nye**

– 17 –

DON'T SHOOT THE
MESSENGER...

The bearer of evil tidings,
When he was halfway there,
Remembered that evil tidings
Were a dangerous thing to bear.
Robert Frost

We will talk about what can happen to the bearer of evil tidings
in a minute. First, though, I want to share some good news.
You may find this totally irrelevant – and perhaps it is – but I
have a reason. More and more I am finding that if I can share
something positive with other people, the act of doing so lifts
my heart. If something pleases me, and I can pass it on to
someone else and it pleases them too, then my day improves.
I can't fix the big things that cause me pain, but I can build in
some small happy things, perhaps, to add some light to all that
shade.

A couple of days ago, I took my dogs for a walk to a different local lake, one we don't go to very often. It occurred to me that I don't go there because Lovely Donald preferred the shorter walk at our usual lake – but the dogs and I only need to consider our own preferences now. As we walked round the lake, a swan came into view, moving quite slowly and lazily. And then, behind her, came seven – seven! – cygnets, learning to be swans. Another adult swan followed behind them – a kind of cygnet sandwich. We watched them until the dogs showed they were getting bored, and then moved on. There's something about cygnets that makes me smile.

And it gets better. Yesterday we went back to the usual lake – actually three small lodges very close together. We saw that the cormorants are back, sitting on the stumps that poke out of the largest of the lodges. They come back every year. Like the cygnets, they are worth watching – their absolute stillness as they sit on their stumps, then suddenly, one dives into the water - a fish! I love its speed and gracefulness as it disappears under water, and then emerges seconds later – always having travelled a much greater distance than seems possible in the time.

As we walked round to the far side of the lodge, there was another swan, a single adult this time, with three cygnets. This bird seems to have nested quite a distance away from the nesting place of Big Daddy and his mate. Seeing them made another perfect little moment in my day.

In times of great sadness, confusion and trouble, it helps me if I remember to look for these perfect moments, notice them as they pass by, hard as it can be to make that effort. They have to be sought out, these positive experiences, but they are always there to be found if I bother to look. Many of the moments that supported me at the time of Murf's death and later in recollection, have centred around kindness. His death, terrible and shattering as it was, taught me something about kindness, and the kindness I received from friends, family, my son's friends and strangers has carried me through when I could not have survived alone. I remember Murf's friend, who drove more than 200 miles to sit with me and Lovely Donald; my friend, who arrived bearing an orchid, and rice pudding. I remember my son's former girlfriend, who tidied his dreadlocks as he lay in the mortuary, so that he could look his best for his funeral. And there was more, much more – people caring that we were in pain and expressing that care. And I had borne the evil tidings of my son's death to all these people. They did not punish me for it.

Murf is dead, and thus has no bond with me or anyone. I am still alive, though, and I have a continuing bond with him, as do his friends and family members and colleagues. That continuing bond with my son is expressed in part through the contact we all have with each other, when memories, anecdotes, happiness and sadness are shared. In this connectedness my son has a kind of life.

I also have a continuing bond with Lovely Donald, of course, but this is more complicated.

It's possible that in writing this I am both trying to resolve this continuing bond with Lovely Donald, lay it to rest, and also trying to make whatever sense can be made of my experience. I am happy for the continuing bond with Murf to continue continuing – I have no need or desire for it to end. Lovely Donald, though, is something else. I need – want – him to become a part of my past. He is inevitably a significant part of my past, but I do not want him to dominate my present or my future. Of course, I realise that perhaps there is no sense to be made of my life with Lovely Donald. As Murf used to say with irritating frequency, we are where we are. Not everything in life makes sense. It seems to me, though, that if I fall into the gap between my life as I believed it to be and my life as it actually was, I may never escape. In the meantime, I can look out for the cygnets, observe the cormorants and enjoy watching my dogs being themselves, all of us completely in the moment.

I don't think I am procrastinating this time, but maybe we do need to get down to some discussion of what it is like to be the bearer of evil tidings.

Sometimes people confuse the message with the messenger, as Robert Frost's protagonist understood when he wisely decided to stay put, make a life, raise a family, forget about delivering his message. It can be dangerous to be the person who delivers bad news, a message people really don't want to hear. Lovely Donald was always going to put me in the position of either having to keep his secrets, whatever it cost me, or else having to tell people what they wouldn't want to know. He chose not to delete messages from his phone and to leave evidence of at least some of his affairs in places where it would inevitably be found after his death. Within all that I could be angry about, what I am very angry about is his lack of care, concern or thought for anyone. After all, it might not have been me who sorted through his belongings after his death. It might have been one of his children – the same children whom he said would be distressed if they knew of his infidelities. They, rather than me, could have opened the file marked SERMONS and found Linda's sad naked photographs and the card with them, removing any doubt that they were intended for Donald. Lovely Donald never did tidy up after himself.

I have already said that I am not innocent and that is true on several levels. I have answered my summons to the Court of Marital Offences and faced the questioning from the judge who presides there. I have to plead guilty to some counts. Occasional inconsistency? Guilty. A quick temper at times and a sharp tongue? Guilty. Expecting more from Lovely Donald than he was capable of giving? Guilty. Being distracted by life from addressing the problems I did perceive? Guilty. Allowing Lovely Donald to fob me off when I did raise issues rather than persevering? Guilty. But these feel like fairly ordinary misdemeanours to me. Do these things justify or even contribute to all Lovely Donald's deceptions over so many years? The jury finds itself unable to reach a verdict.

When I had Donald's phone in my possession in those first days, I did not search through it for other messages. What else did I need to see, after all? So I had done nothing wrong at that point, beyond being oblivious to the possibility of deceit.

In the six weeks that followed, Donald remained in hospital, and I continued to visit, almost automatically. Perhaps I was still a wife bot. We had many conversations about what I had seen on his phone, and it became increasingly apparent that Lovely Donald was lying about what had happened, unable, perhaps in his weakened state, to maintain his usual skill in deception. He did not like questions, and liked even less those times I pointed out the contradictions and impossibilities in his answers. Sometimes I was sad; sometimes I was angry; always I was confused. Once I got drunk enough to avoid thinking or feeling anything. It didn't help.

If I am to be honest now, I have to confess that I gave him a harder time than was, perhaps, appropriate for someone as ill as he proved to be. I did argue with him, point out the holes – miles wide – in his story, highlight the contradictions, demand answers. I ask myself now whether there was any point to any of this.

I tried to be fair. I accepted that I had not been a perfect wife – maybe not even an adequate wife, at times. Lovely Donald begged and begged me not to leave, not to tell anyone, not to take the dogs if I did leave… And I told him that if we were to have any possibility of any kind of future, I needed total honesty. One more lie, I said, and I would be gone. Whatever the truth, however hurtful it might be, however destructive I might find it, it was preferable to more lies. I gave him second, third, fourth, umpteenth chances to be honest… *Speak truths not lies*. He didn't listen, preferring, it seems, to listen to Friend Dick's contention that it was best to tell as little of the truth as possible. In seeking the truth, said Friend Dick, I was failing to understand my own interests, which would best be served by knowing as little about Donald's past affairs as possible. I should now focus on looking after Lovely Donald, making sure his needs were met. (A friend likened this to the mushroom theory of marriage – keep your wife in the dark and shovel shit on her.)

I could have tried to be forgiving if Lovely Donald had expressed any guilt or remorse or empathy for my situation. If I could have felt he was striving for honesty. Nothing. Nothing at all. His concern was all about how other people would regard him if they knew the truth. His relationship with Linda was helpful for all of us, he said, because it saved him from his much riskier relationships with prostitutes. It only lasted two years, he said. It was 'never going anywhere'. 'We were using each other.' He couldn't leave me because he 'had nowhere to go' and his sons would have lost respect for him. Our son would have sided with me. I wouldn't have let him take the dogs if he'd left. He would have lost the contact with my family, who had become his family over the years. He was, in any case, *entitled* to some excitement in his life. It was all over now, anyway. He'd been completely faithful for the last three years as his worsening health destroyed his libido, and these had been the happiest years of his life... And – my favourite – I was better company than Linda, he said, because he could have an intelligent conversation about politics with me, and I would watch *Question Time* on TV with him and have opinions about the issues raised, whereas Linda had no interest in politics, no intellectual interests at all, in fact. I am lost behind the looking glass, in a surreal world of distorted images...

But – I am not innocent. Six weeks to the day from finding that text, I did something that still gives me a sense of shame even now, months later. Lovely Donald asked me to pay a bill online for him. In order to do so, I had to go into his email account to get the password I needed to be able to pay the bill – Lovely Donald had forgotten it. So far, so good – I went, at his request, to get the password. I got it, paid the bill, but then – and here is where the shamefulness comes in – I went back. I typed Lollipop Linda's name into the SEARCH box in his email account. Pages of emails came up, covering many more than two years. I had no desire to read them all. I clicked on one at random – 'I am filing our emails,' it said, 'in the file called America. Nobody will ever look there.'

I didn't read them all – why would I? I read some from the beginning, a couple from the middle and some from the end. They covered some nine years. The earliest one I read mentioned events that had happened two years earlier than that – so an eleven-year relationship, then. Or more – I never did quite nail down the exact duration of the affair with Lovely Linda. It depends what you mean by *affair*, I suppose. Some comments felt gratuitously unkind – 'Hattie and I are going on holiday,' wrote Lovely Donald, 'I need to book us into a cottage that sleeps eight so we can avoid each other as much as possible…' And yet he talked often about how much he enjoyed those holidays in Cherry Cottage. Where does the truth lie? Don't ask me.

I confronted Lovely Donald. I should not have read the emails, he said. They were not written for me. He was completely right; they weren't written for me. I had no right to read them.

Here's a moral and ethical conundrum. I needed to know the truth in order to know what to do. I knew Lovely Donald was lying. Was I entitled to use whatever means I could to find out what had been going on behind the façade of the good man? Was I entitled to know the truth about my own life? I feel shame that I read the emails. I would probably do the same thing again in the same circumstances. What, I wonder, would you have done?

I had a lot to think about. Leaving Lovely Donald inevitably meant losing my home – he was not going to be well enough for the strain of finding somewhere and moving out and, unlike him, I have family I could go to. It probably meant losing my dogs, since it was unlikely I could take them with me. (My family likes cats! Cats and terriers aren't a good mix.) I would certainly lose what financial security I had. Lovely Donald and his Lindas have stolen a lot from me one way and another, and could now put me into a financially precarious situation. What to do? I wished I was younger, fitter, able to return to work… '*If wishes were horses, beggars would ride*,' I hear my mother's voice saying.

I struggled, too, with Donald's repeated contention that the last three, faithful years had been the happiest of his life – impotence had forced him into fidelity, but he had felt the better for it, he said.

These were the years we had watched our son suffer, to the point where he could struggle no more and ended his life. Happy? Buffering…

I dithered. I was worried about my stepsons. And others. I did not want to hurt or potentially damage people by revealing the extent of Lovely Donald's deception. Family and friends had trusted him, believed in him, shared their secrets with him, loved him, even, and accepted him for whom they believed him to be. How could I shatter their sense of trust in him? How could I not? Buffering...

I dithered. Lovely Donald was very ill by this point – the result both of his failure over many years to regulate his appetites and also of his refusal forever to tell the truth about his various symptoms to any of the doctors he had seen. Whilst he was not imminently dying (I thought), it was unlikely he would live very long. He would need help with day-to-day living and could I in all conscience just walk away and leave him to struggle? Leave my stepson to struggle with him? Buffering...

I dithered. I knew, by this time, that Linda was one of a group of Lindas rather than just a single individual. I knew that some kind of relationship with the Ultimate Linda, Lady of the Lollipop, had continued, off and on, over some eleven to fifteen years. I knew about Lovely Donald's penchant for internet dating sites for married people looking for co-adulterers. I knew there were also non-sexual, emotional affairs, such as an online relationship with a woman called Stephanie. I didn't know as much as I know now, but I knew enough. I knew, too, that Lovely Donald seemed to be prepared to continue to lie, to try to cover up, to do anything rather than be honest... buffering...

What I didn't know then, and what Lovely Donald knew all too well, was that my belief that he had always shown care and commitment to his children was also a lie. He must have realised that he could no longer prevent my stepsons and their mother and I from having a real conversation and that if we did, more revelations would result for all of us... The Lovely Donald mask would become even more tarnished. I can feel some sadness for him, for the absolute fear he must have felt.

I felt trapped. I *was* trapped. My image is of myself enmeshed in a sticky web of spider silk, with something dark and destructive coming ever closer... Lovely Donald must have been feeling something similar...

I confided in one of Lovely Donald's consultants, who was being kinder to me than I could bear, talking about my thirty-four-year marriage and how hard it must be for me now... He did not advise me – how could he? He did say that Lovely Donald was not going to live long. Medically, there were few options left. The damage was too great. Maybe I should not walk away at this point? How would I feel later if I did walk away? Donald was going to need help; we had been together a long time. Who else would offer the help needed? Was it wise to put myself in a precarious financial situation by leaving now? He thought of most of the questions I was asking myself. He missed the one that said, 'Why should I allow Donald and his women to cause me even more harm?' And the one where I tried to quantify the harm to me from leaving against the harm to me from staying.

The doctor had thought Donald still had a little time. Donald, facing a future of failing physical health, physical limitations and flooded watertight compartments, maybe saw little to live for, and he made his own choices. All the Lindas had disappeared as surely as if they had never existed. The Ultimate Linda, now in a new relationship with a widower, was not coming to Donald's rescue any time soon. Having invested little emotion or commitment into his family, Donald now found himself with only his family to rely on. How bleak that must have felt. I had said to him that he had invested in the wrong woman. I wonder if he reflected on that as he lay in his hospital bed? As I write this, I find myself weeping, not entirely for myself.

When I was called into the hospital early one morning, Lovely Donald's monitor showed that his heart rate, pulse and oxygen levels were all satisfactory. He was breathing, but had retreated into the liminal place between life and death. 'His numbers are good,' said the doctor, 'but he is dying. He has given up.' And so he died, with his elder son and I by his bed, and his younger son joining us via the miracle of smartphone technology. His friend, another clergyman, gave him the last rites. He died peacefully and without struggle. No need for medication. I felt he had made a choice, and I wondered, as I saw him take a final breath and come to a gentle stop, whether he had made this choice for me and his sons as well as for himself. Had he survived, I wondered, what could our lives have been?

Donald's 'numbers were good', the doctor had said, but he died anyway. The cause of death on his death certificate was a urinary tract infection that had arisen because of problems with his catheter. And this was happening in the context of multiorgan failure – his lungs, heart and kidneys were all weakened by his refusal to make any modifications to his diet or alcohol consumption, despite having Type 2 diabetes. Like many people, he'd always looked for a quick fix for his weight issues – a pill, a miracle diet – and none of the quick fixes had worked, unsurprisingly. Some had probably been harmful. He'd also worked for thirty-two years as a night-duty social worker, and the negative consequences of shift work for health are well documented. Life caught up with him at the last.

I think he'd always believed he was unsinkable in more ways than one – that somehow he could escape any negative consequences from an unhealthy diet and a tendency to binge-drink. And after all, he's not alone in this and nor is he alone in his refusal to seek medical advice or to follow it when he couldn't avoid it. Nonetheless, I felt that there was something willed in his death on that day. As the consultant said, he'd given up on life. He'd have realised that I was about to find him out in yet another lie, and I don't think he could face the inevitable consequences of the choices and decisions he'd made. Perhaps death, at this point, felt like an escape? Like the easier option?

I felt – and still feel – what? Sadness for all his wasted potential. Relief that I was spared a decision that I knew, deep down, could only go one way. I could not have lived with Lovely Donald. Even more important, he could not have lived with himself. The gap between the self he was and the self he pretended, maybe even wanted, to be was too great. His fall into that gap was not survivable.

I was the bearer of evil tidings in many different ways.

Lovely Donald saw through my eyes how his actions over years would look to other people. He saw, perhaps, that beyond himself and Friend Dick, no one else in our circle would consider him *entitled* to his secret life. He saw through my eyes, and felt shame, and the realisation that people would feel differently towards him, would see behind the Lovely Donald mask to what lay beneath it. Even worse, perhaps, I brought him the news that the control he believed himself to have over everyone and everything was an illusion. He was not invincible, untouchable. I had learned his secrets by accident; he had not prevented this from happening. He was not in control. It was possible that other people might learn his secrets, by accident or because I revealed them. If he was, as I speculated earlier, tired of all the deception anyway, this was not in his conscious awareness. There was a sense of panic in his realisation that his belief that he could keep the different areas of his life in watertight compartments was a foolish belief, a delusion. He gripped my hand, fearful as a young child in a thunderstorm. I pitied him, despite everything.

I was the bearer of evil tidings for many people. I was the person bringing news of Donald's illness, its seriousness, his deteriorating prognosis and eventually, his death. People were, according to their lights and in their own individual ways, uniformly kind and supportive of me. I was grateful for their kindness.

Then, too, as the impossibility of keeping Lovely Donald's secrets became increasingly apparent, as people who know me began to question me, to speculate that maybe I was more seriously ill than I had admitted, or maybe struggling financially, or going under in one way or another, I became the bearer of evil tidings once again. People knew Lovely Donald well, knew his virtues and his faults, his strengths and his failings, the person he was. Except they didn't.

Most people were, as before, uniformly kind and supportive. For one or two people, though, the burden of even a bowdlerised version of the truth was too much. They were angry with me for speaking ill of the dead, for defacing their 'Lovely Donald' icon and, in at least one case, for obviously being the kind of person who must have driven Lovely Donald into the arms of internet pick-ups in the first place. Is that true? I'm honestly not sure. Maybe. Perhaps. Possibly. But probably not.

I have to carry the weight not only of the evil tidings, but also the weight of delivering those tidings and their impact on the people to whom I delivered them. I know very well that I am not responsible for Donald's actions or the consequences of those actions, but I am the person who has to live those consequences and tidy up the mess. Never have I wished so much that I could be a better liar. I have to pay attention to my motivations too, because if I expose Lovely Donald's secrets out of a desire for revenge, I will be contaminated by that. I have struggled to tread a path of right actions, and I have stumbled and made missteps along the way.

I have, at times, found myself uncertain about what was real and what was a product of my imagination. I became convinced that a friend and my stepson both knew of Lovely Donald's affairs – they didn't. Both had been talking about other things, some already known to me, others not. The impossibility of finding a path through these choking weeds and brambles has impeded my sleep, weighed heavily on me whilst awake and sometimes almost choked me. As always, I remind myself to breathe, focus on the movement of my breath in my body, allow the thoughts to come and go, not follow them in futile circles. Breathing in… breathing out… All I can do is make the best decisions I can, and, once made, let go of the choices I didn't take because they have gone. I have done what I have done.

There is a price to be paid for being the bearer of evil tidings, as Lovely Donald himself recognised. 'I've put you in an impossible situation,' he said, 'you are such a rubbish liar'. That was the nearest he came to any kind of apology or regret. I wish I could have had the option available to Robert Frost's protagonist:

> 'As for his evil tidings,
> Belshazzar's overthrow,
> Why hurry to tell Belshazzar
> What soon enough he would know?'

In fact, I did have that option. I considered moving far away, where nobody would know me or Lovely Donald and nobody would ask questions. I considered the possibility that I could cut myself off, as far as possible, from everyone I know.

But, as they say in the movies, 'you can run, but you can't hide', and the truth floats up like oil on water.

– 18 –

IT'S LIFE, JIM, BUT NOT AS WE KNOW IT...

My mind has given me images and metaphors to help me to process my emotions as I try to find a way to live my life from now, adjust to the new realities. Collapsing ice shelves, frozen oceans, death in the vacuum of deep space, being lost in the jungle, leeches and clowns – all of these have felt very real to me as I have wandered through these words and worlds. My clown make-up was itchy and uncomfortable. The happy clown face and the sad clown face were masks, reflecting only a partial reality. I could feel their itchiness on my skin.

Throughout it all the dragons have been offstage, heard occasionally but seen only from the corner of my eye and indistinctly, as if through gauze or fog. Don't forget the dragons – they are important – but they aren't quite ready to appear in their full reality. My dragon-whispering skills need more work before the dragons and I can talk to each other. They are waiting, biding their time. They want, I realise, to communicate with me, not to destroy me. They do not regard me as lunch. We will know when it is their time, when they will come onstage in all their dragon strength and energy. Not yet, but soon.

I can try to block out my experiences, my emotions, my thoughts, as when I remove my space helmet and escape life, or focus on practicalities, become the wife bot, emotionless, robotic. I speculated earlier that I spent thirty-four years with Lovely Donald singing to myself to drown out my warning bells, to impose a version of reality that suited me at the time. It takes a lot of effort to block life, thoughts, feelings – it is hard and tiring, and requires an ultimately destructive kind of endurance. This is true physically, mentally and emotionally.

There is a balance I have to find here. Physically, the reality of my illness means that sometimes I just have to accept pain, exhaustion and discomfort as the background to my day – but the dogs still have to be walked and I still have to take basic care of myself and my surroundings. I have to bring myself to a point of balance, where I do enough to sustain all of us and avoid becoming deconditioned, but not so much that I drain myself to the point of collapse. This holds as true for living with emotional earthquakes as for living with illness. It has been a lesson for me to learn that when I talk about 'doing my best', there is, in fact, no absolute *best* that I can do. My best today may be more – or less – than my best tomorrow. I have to know myself and my body, accept imperfection, allow 'good enough' to be good enough. It is harder than it sounds. I am not always very good at it.

So, of course, I don't always find that point of balance, that sweet spot. When I miss it, hardening against my experience until the blocking becomes too much to sustain, the inevitable reaction is that I can abandon myself to inertia, to a sense of helplessness and powerlessness. I can drown, as when I drank two bottles of wine in a sitting or abandoned myself to the leeches. Again I need to look for the point of balance. I have to know that I still have a choice. I can lie down and give up, or I can face what needs to be faced, look the dragons squarely in the eye. I can, in other words, choose to help myself first – and then, maybe, I will find other helpers to support me. Then, too, I will be able to see the helpers who have been supporting me all the time – avian, canine and human – rather than allowing their support and care to go unnoticed and unvalued.

I can start from where I am – where else could I start from? – and I can put one foot in front of the other, a step at a time. What other choice is there, after all? This is all about choices. I can choose to harden into coldness, hardness, bitterness, rage, even. I can choose to dissolve into misery and bewail the unfairness of life. Curse God and die, or crawl into a pit of helplessness and abandon hope. I do have a choice – I know I have a choice – so I choose to focus on the point of balance.

I am not alone. Grief remains my ever-present companion, but I have other companions too. Hardening and wallowing will both happen from time to time – that's life. But again I have a choice, once I recognise where I am going, to continue down that path… or stop. Take a moment – breathe – stand outside the thoughts and feelings a little bit rather than becoming consumed by them. Is this the way I really want to go? All things are passing and this too will pass, if I allow it to pass rather than clinging on to it. If I remember to breathe…

And where am I going now? The imagined reality my mind has taken me to feels like the most improbable one of all. But it is where my inner voice – too often ignored – is telling me that I need to go.

It is February 2018. I am sitting in a room in the hospital with Lovely Donald and his doctors, a nurse, and a social worker, a physiotherapist and an occupational therapist. We are planning his discharge from hospital. Obviously he didn't die then, because here he is, large as life. My stepson cannot join us – he has to go to work – but has agreed to visit later for an update from Donald and from me. The doctor is available this evening, and will come back to talk to him if he wishes.

The physiotherapist has managed to improve Lovely Donald's mobility beyond expectations. He can manage stairs if he takes his time. She thinks he will manage a short walk with the dogs if I am there to hold on to the leads. The occupational therapist has been back to the house, advised how to maximise Donald's chances of managing at home, where to put his bed etc., etc. She confirms that Donald can manage his own personal care if he takes his time. She thinks it would be good for him to take on small tasks, like doing the washing-up, rather than just sitting in a chair all day. The social worker has talked to Donald on the ward, and has been to see me too. He is concerned that my health compromises my ability to help Lovely Donald, and suggests that we might benefit from arranging for carers to

come in, even if only once a day. Donald isn't keen on this –
nor am I, if truth be told. We agree to see how we manage first,
and talk again with the social worker when Donald has been
back at home for a couple of weeks.

We all know – the consultant has been clear and honest
– that Lovely Donald is far from well. His heart, lungs and
kidneys are all damaged. However, the efforts he has made
to lose a serious amount of weight while maintaining an
adequately healthy diet have paid off. Maybe Lovely Donald
can have a little more time with a reasonably good quality of
life. Maybe, the doctor suggests, we could plan a holiday? We
could both do with a break, she thinks.

This is the version of the multiverse in which Donald, once
I found his 'lollipop' text message, expressed remorse, told
me, honestly and openly, what had happened over the years.
Talked about how he had blocked off any sense of wrongdoing
to justify to himself his need to escape from the constraints of
domesticity and family life. He has talked to a therapist about
his need to break the rules, see himself as above the ordinary
conventions that govern most of us. He has talked, too, about
his need for a transgressive sex life, what that might be about.
I am not present during these conversations with the therapist
but they seem to be helping. Lovely Donald seems calmer,
more at peace with himself. He has been able to talk to his sons
openly about how and why he let them down in the past. He
has been able to open the remaining watertight compartments
for himself, and so has not been swamped and sunk. He can
face the hurt he has brought to his sons, to me, to our dead

son (who had, perhaps, confronted him years ago about the dating websites seen in his web-browsing history when our son was fixing his father's laptop). Lovely Donald lied to our son, and could only now face and admit the lie. He thought he had succeeded in reassuring our son – who never said any more about any of it to anyone – that the dating sites had been an accident, never followed up. I hope so.

I am not sure that Lovely Donald and I can live together – I will always be Hoodwinked Hattie, after all – but I understand that thirty-four years is a long time, a lot of history. Donald and I are the only people who can understand what it felt like to be our son's parents. We planned his funeral. Beside that, Linda seems trivial.

As we approached our meeting with the hospital staff providing Donald's care, I made a choice to try to house share, at least. We will continue to walk the dogs and watch *Question Time* and do the *Guardian* crossword – the small routines of everyday life. Lovely Donald will go out for fresh bagels every Sunday morning. He has agreed to keep his own space clean and tidy and work, after discharge, on reducing his paper mountain in the house. He has told me about the naked photographs of the Lovely Lollipop Lady Linda, and the other mementos of his Dark Side, and expressed the intention to find all this stuff, once he gets home, and add it to the pile to be fed to my incinerator.

We tiptoe carefully around each other. He is not the man I thought he was, and I know that. He will not be physically unfaithful again, because age and ill-health have removed the possibility of physical affairs and eroded his desire to seek out emotional affairs. Is this enough? No, not really. I would like to feel that he had made a positive choice to commit himself to his marriage, his family. But there is no way to know whether he would have chosen fidelity had infidelity been possible. He has, as far as I can tell, made the full and frank disclosure that I asked for when I gave him back his phone. He says that we can build on this. I am doubtful, at best. But do either of us really want to have to start again at our age, in our state of health? And – ever Practical Hattie as well as Hoodwinked Hattie – what would we do with the dogs?

Lovely Donald has talked about the possibility that he and Friend Dick brought out the worst in each other, reinforced each other's self-justifications and dishonesties. We have even joked (a little and carefully) about the mushroom theory of marriage. Lovely Donald has said that he did not confide in anyone other than Friend Dick because, he realises now, none of his other friends would have given him the feedback that he was *entitled* to have affairs. Perhaps, he speculates, his relationship with Friend Dick might have been unwholesome for both of them? I agree that this might well be the case. He has noticed how, in the twenty years of his friendship with Dick, he has allowed other friendships to lapse. Why?, he wonders. I don't know.

The doctor suggests that we plan a discharge date a few days hence. We talk about how Lovely Donald will be followed up by the various professionals. They seem optimistic. There is a feeling of cautious hope around us all…

And now I am losing patience.

Are you finding any of this even remotely plausible? Convincing? Could Lovely Donald, at the age of seventy, have chosen to embrace truthfulness? Have chosen to talk openly to me, his sons, maybe even his ex-wife? Could he ever have given up his dreadful diet and dysfunctional relationship with alcohol? Is any of this happening in any part of the multiverse?

Could I seriously have contemplated continuing to live in the same house with him? Continued to cook his lunch? Help him with the crossword? Discuss *Question Time*? Lovely Linda, and all the other Lindas, just a regrettable part of the past, a mistake, but something to be forgiven and forgotten? I'd welcome your thoughts. I'm struggling here.

You must remember, too, that whilst I am trying to be as honest as I can in what I write, I am still bound and limited by my own consciousness, my personality and perceptions and emotions. Lovely Donald, had he chosen to be honest, would have had his own story to tell. Undoubtedly, it would have looked and sounded very different from mine.

One thing he did say was that a big reason he hadn't wanted to end our marriage was his realisation that it was not his relationship with me that was the problem, any more than it was his relationship with his first wife that had been the problem in his first marriage. The problem, he said, lay in his relationship with himself, and all the problems that had surfaced for him in both his marriages would have surfaced again in any relationship with any woman, even Long-term Lovely Lollipop Lady Linda, if they had lived together. Having a wife at home (to blame?) and a 'loving friendship' with a non-driver living fifty miles away suited him perfectly, he said. He could enjoy his relationship with Linda without fear that she would turn up at some inconvenient moment, and without disrupting his everyday life. He did not, as far as I could tell, see anything questionable or wrong in this, though it seemed to me that he saw women, maybe other people in general, only in relation to his own wants and needs rather than as individuals in their own right.

BUT – he has no opportunity now to tell his story in his own way. He missed the moment when that was possible, so missing, perhaps, a kind of redemption. But am I imposing my own world view again here? I would hate to feel that I was telling lies on my deathbed, but I have no idea how Lovely Donald felt. I do not know his story. I do not know what he felt or believed to be truth. Speculation is just speculation.

I find it easier to believe that I was lost in space than to believe that Lovely Donald could ever have given me a straightforward account of what happened, changed his diet or apologised. Despite being a therapist himself, he had always managed to avoid being in therapy. 'I don't need therapy,' he used to say, and I have no reason to believe that he would have changed his mind about this. I don't think I could have found a way to continue to live with him, whatever the problems caused by leaving might have been.

But I could be wrong. I've been wrong before, after all.

HIATUS (2)

I have been a meditator since my late teens, so for more than forty years now. I was taught the basics of what I now know as mindfulness when I was seventeen, and it has been a support through my life. I have neglected regular practice for weeks and months at a time, and sometimes even for years, but I have always come back to it. Now, together with Grief, it has become my daily companion. Mindfulness of grief helps me to meet it and move with it and through it. Fighting grief, suppressing it, refusing to face it wouldn't help. Grief isn't going away. But if I walk with it, face it, acknowledge it, then life can send a few green shoots to grow around the grief. Grief won't leave, but Life will walk with me and my dogs too.

How does mindfulness help me? Let me count the ways. The nature of my illness means that I am clumsy. If I don't focus my awareness on what I am doing in the moment when chopping carrots, for example, I am liable to find myself chopping fingers. When I am walking, I am walking – if I fail to maintain my awareness of my feet, then I may well be tripping or falling. So mindfulness in daily life helps me to keep my balance – literally – and keeps me out of A&E.

It also helps me to maintain my metaphorical balance too, to cultivate equanimity. Equanimity – my favourite word in the English language. Don't you think it is a beautiful word? Just try saying it and listen to the sound it makes. Equanimity. It is defined in the Oxford English Dictionary as 'calmness and composure, especially in a difficult situation', from the Latin aequus, meaning equal, and animus, meaning mind. So, an equal or balanced mind that is neither seeking to block out experience nor being overwhelmed by it. It's a goal, at least, something to work towards day by day.

A part of my daily meditation practice is a meditation on compassion. I can spend as little as ten minutes on this, or as long as an hour. It depends how I feel, how much time I have, how difficult I'm finding it...

I begin by holding my own self in my awareness, in my mind's eye, with love and with compassion for my sufferings and appreciation for my joys. Sometimes this is hard to do. If I can't quite manage it, I can focus on having the intention to feel compassion and the intention to remember that there are good things amongst all the other stuff.

Then I move my awareness to a friend, someone for whom it is easy to have feelings of regard and well-wishing. I focus, too, on what I share with my friend – our shared desire to avoid suffering, to be happy, and our shared experience of the breath.

And then I release my friend and bring my awareness to a neutral person, someone I've seen but don't know, so have no real feelings about, either positive or negative. So I bring into my awareness, for example, the woman who served me when I went to buy milk and a newspaper, wishing her well, reflecting on our common experiences...

And then I gather my awareness and focus on a person I find difficult or irritating, or maybe someone who has harmed me in some way, or harmed people I care about...

The driver who cut me up on the M60... the dog walker who allowed his dog to terrorise my little Jack Russell... The Lady of the Lollipops, Friend Dick, Lovely Donald...

And now I'm struggling. Yesterday I managed to feel compassion and well- wishing for the careless driver without too much of a struggle. It was harder, on Tuesday, to feel those feelings towards the man with the aggressive dog, but I held on to the intention to feel compassion and well-wishing towards him and his dog, to wish them healing.

When I tried to bring in the Lollipop Lady the other day, it was more difficult again, so again I focused on having the intention to wish her well... it was a thin shadow of an intention, almost invisible, but it was there.

And then I come to Friend Dick and Lovely Donald, and I am defeated. I'm aware of my intention slithering and sliding away from me. I examine what I am thinking and feeling. I am not wishing them ill, wanting harm to come to them (though maybe it is a bit late for Lovely Donald), and I can feel some compassion for their sufferings, their lack of awareness. And that, it seems, is the best I can do for now.

And I am not failing. There is no wrong way to meditate. This is where I am right now, in this moment. Struggling. A flicker of irritation creeps in – what did they care for my experience, *my suffering? I notice it and let it go. There is no wrong way to feel. We feel what we feel. We think what we think. The bit we can control is what we do, our behaviour. I have felt murderous rage towards all three of these people who damaged me and, even worse, damaged my son… but I don't have to act on that murderous rage and I don't have to live in it. I can have the intention to let it go, even if I can't quite manage that just yet for every minute of every day… Ultimately I can be almost free of it, for the sake of my own wellbeing. I can't change the past, much as I might wish to do so. Unfortunately, we don't have any PAUSE – REWIND buttons. But I don't have to let the past destroy my here and now or my future. Resentment, hatred, bitterness, regret – who will be harmed if I dwell in these feelings? As the Buddha said, what we dwell on, we become. At this moment, though, I have no particular desire to wish Lovely Donald, Lollipop Linda and Friend Dick well. Having the intention to let go of rage and to let go of any desire to inflict on them some measure of the harm they inflicted on me and mine – letting go of all that is the best I can do right now.*

I move my awareness to my son, difficult, at times, in life but his absence is wrenching in every second of every day. My son is not here, but his legacy in the world is a good one. He is remembered with love and kindness by many, many people. Many people have talked of his positive influence in their lives. He made his own choices, for his own reasons. He has a story worth telling – but not here and not now. He was driven to his death, in part, by someone else's malice, but we can talk about that another time. For now, focus on his life. Focus on warmth, love, kindness… And we only really know kindness when we live with loss.

Just breathe into the feeling… focus on the intention to feel a loving awareness of our connectedness with all life, even Friend Dick and Lovely Donald. I will return to them individually another day. For now I can just have a general feeling of well-wishing towards all life, in the air, on the earth and in the oceans.

For now, Breathe…

– 19 –

'I HAVE A DARK SIDE...'

'I have a dark side,' said Lovely Donald. Repeatedly.

I have a dark side too. Maybe we all do? Maybe where we differ individually is the degree to which we allow our dark side to dominate us? That assumes, of course, that we have a choice, some degree of free will. I remember my son telling me about experiments in neuroscience that suggest our brain patterns show that our brain begins to initiate an action before we develop any conscious intention to carry out that action. Does this undermine notions of free will? As far as I can tell from my limited knowledge of the issues, scientists and philosophers are still slugging it out. Whether or not we have free will, something I heard the other day on the radio suggests that it might be a good idea to continue to believe that we have it. Some studies of moral behaviour have apparently shown that in situations where an ethical choice has to be made (about cheating in a test), the people who believe in free will behave more ethically than the people who don't believe in it. In other words, if you believe you have a choice about your actions, then you are more likely to choose to behave ethically in any given situation. Is it relevant that both Linda and Lovely Donald talked about having no choice about their behaviour? One of the tenets of mindfulness is that we cannot control everything that happens in our lives, but we can choose how we respond to what happens. Perhaps if you don't know that, or don't believe it, it is easier to think that you can do nothing other than follow the promptings of your wants and desires and emotions? Lovely Donald 'had to' follow his dark side; Lollipop Linda 'had to' pursue their affair. Though it all sounds to me like an excuse for poor behaviour. But what do I know?

Lovely Donald had a great interest in Native American culture and beliefs, and there is an old and maybe too well-known Cherokee legend about the two wolves. You have probably heard it before, but I'm going to tell it again here just in case you don't know it. And because I want to tell it.

A young Cherokee boy has been hurt by an injustice done to him by someone he had believed to be a friend. Struggling with his feelings of anger, resentment, hurt and the desire for revenge, he goes to his grandfather for help. His grandfather tells him a story. 'I too,' he says, 'have been hurt by unkindness and injustice and bad faith. I have felt great anger, even hatred, towards people who have harmed me and haven't even been sorry for the damage they've done. That hatred has exhausted me and ground me down, but hasn't touched the person who hurt me. I have struggled with such feelings many times,' the grandfather continued, 'and it has felt as if two wolves were doing battle inside me. One wolf tries to be kind and loving, and do no harm. He seeks to understand and to live in harmony with all life. He fights only when it is right and necessary to do so. The other wolf is angry all the time, filled with resentment about the least injury, real or imagined. His anger makes him vicious and unhappy, so that he cannot think clearly or find any peace. It can be awfully hard to have these two wolves struggling for dominance inside me...'

'But, Grandfather,' says the boy, 'which wolf will win?'

'The wolf I feed,' says the Grandfather, smiling.

I know it is probably a cliché, but it's a pretty good story, don't you think?

I have wrestled with the slipperiness of truth and reality and perception, and I am also wrestling with what I know or think I know or believe I know about choice and free will. And – God! – it's complicated.

I am choosing, as much as I can, to feed the 'positive wolf' – or at least I think I am. Of course, if I never fed the raging wolf, it would soon die – so it follows that there are times when it gains ground in the struggle and I throw it a bone or a few doggy treats. But I do feel like I have a choice, and when I find myself dwelling on thoughts of hatred and revenge, I ask myself whether this is who I want to be. Most of the time, the answer is *no*. So I shift the focus of my attention. Look away now if you are offended by my occasional biblical quotes.

'Finally, brethren, whatsoever things are true, whatsoever things *are* honest, whatsoever things *are* just, whatsoever things *are* pure, whatsoever things *are* lovely, whatsoever things *are* of good report; if *there be* any virtue, and if *there be* any praise, think on these things.' *Philippians 4:8*

It has been suggested to me that Lovely Donald had an addictive personality, if such a thing exists, and his relationship with food, tobacco and alcohol gives some credence to this suggestion. Is it possible, then, that he was also addicted to transgressive sex, transgressive relationships, the adrenalin buzz of illicit affairs? Addicted to deceit? He was certainly very clear that he had felt no guilt about his visits to massage parlours, but only a great fear of the negative consequences that could follow if he were found out – he imagined the headlines in the local press should he be caught out in a police raid on a brothel. I tend to think that he magnified the risks involved, for reasons of his own about which I can only speculate, but it seems to have been a worry for him. I asked if it had occurred to him to stop going to the massage parlours, and thus remove all risk. I never really got a reply to what might, after all, have been a stupid question. Of course the only way he could stop was to find a woman to have an affair with – no other choice seemed to have been imaginable for him.

So Lovely Donald decided that internet dating sites for married people and secret affairs were a safer option than brothels – Linda was, in fact, by her willingness to enter into a long-term affair with him, doing us all a favour, saving him from the risks of massage parlours and saving us, his family, from the risk of the public embarrassment of having him caught in a police raid. It all makes sense, doesn't it, from his frame of reference?

Is this addiction? And, if it is, does the addictive nature of the behaviours remove all choice? Could Lovely Donald have done nothing other than what he did? He couldn't help himself? He had no choice? But then some people become *recovering* addicts, don't they? They presumably make a difficult choice to try, one day at a time, not to feed the wolf of their addiction. So doesn't that mean that even addicts make choices?

I am in my own personal cloud of unknowing. I've said this before, and I might end up saying it again later – answers, if you have them, on a postcard, please.

I'm going to pause in a minute so that I can go and feed my dogs (not the wolves). There's another wolf around for me, and this one is all too easy for me to feed. His name is Despair, and he's been prowling around today. The loss of a child is a heavy loss, beside which all else becomes smaller. Despair will pad beside me sometimes, his grey head heavy, as he walked around the lake with us this morning. I accept him with Grief as an inevitable companion. He's wandered off now, for the time being. He'll be back. In the meantime, my terriers are hungry. They are telling me to feed them – now, please! And then we will return to my own 'Dark Side Wolf'.

– 20 –

DON'T YOU MAMAGUY ME...!

I wake up and am immediately alert. All around me are the familiar sounds of the rainforest – no hoots of alarm or warning at this moment, I note with relief. I am, I realise, sitting in a tree, lush, green leaves surrounding me, fruit within easy reach. I feel a sharp nudge in the small of my back, and a voice scolds in my ear, 'How can I groom you if you won't sit still? Stop wriggling!'

I know this voice, but I can't quite call the speaker into my mind's eye. I turn to have a look who it is. Of course! It is my grandmother – how could I not have realised? And she's a baboon – no, not a baboon. A monkey. A mandrill! And naturally this must mean that I'm a mandrill too. When did that happen? Why didn't I notice? Do I like this better than I liked being a clown? Maybe. I'm not sure.

I look around me, seeing the almost entirely female mandrill horde that forms my community. I see only juvenile males, no adults. I remember that the adult males go off to their own places, away from here, returning only for a short time during the breeding season. Maybe life is calmer without them. We females look out for each other and care for each other's young ones. This is a good life, with only the occasional leopard, snake or bushmeat hunter to worry about. There are no threats around today, though, so we can relax into the tasks of socialising, child-rearing and finding food. This is a good day. It will pass, as all days do, good and bad alike, but I can relax into it for now.

I like this grooming thing. It feels pleasurable. My grandmother's careful fingers comb through my fur, removing parasites and soothing my skin. I close my eyes and enjoy the moment while it lasts. 'Right,' she says, 'you're done.' And off she goes, moving laterally up the canopy, going, no doubt, to chat to her friends with their usual combination of complaint and one-upmanship as they discuss their grandchildren…

I look around me, feeling at home here. But of course, I will look around me again and, in the unpredictable moment, I will find myself somewhere else.

And so it proves. I am back in my kitchen, looking through my emails. Every day I get an email from *Oxford Dictionaries* with their word of the day. It's fun, and sometimes I learn a new word. Whatever shape the day takes on, reading the word of the day is a small pleasure. I need to take these small pleasures where I can find them, after all.

The word of the day a few days ago was 'mamaguy', a word I'd never come across before.

Mamaguy:

West Indian

Try to deceive (someone), especially with flattery or untruths.
'Don't try to mamaguy me at all!'

Origin

From Spanish mamar gallo *'make a monkey of'.*

Despite its negative meaning, it is a word that makes me smile. It has a pleasant sound – *mamaguy*. Maybe the word itself reflects its meaning, deceiving with flattery or untruths, its pleasing sound diluting its unpleasant connotations.

I wonder if Lovely Donald knew this word?

NOTE TO READER

I am, of course, assuming that you have stayed with me. I hope so. It's good to have company sometimes.

It's interesting – when I started to write this, I was writing it for myself, with no thought of showing it to anyone else apart from the inevitable therapist I am seeing. But as time has gone by, I've felt more and more that I am writing for anonymous others as well as for myself. I wonder whether, once you begin to write, it becomes increasingly necessary to imagine a reader?

I've asked myself whether in writing this I am taking a kind of revenge on Lovely Donald and Friend Dick. I don't think so. I hope not. Why not revenge on Lollipop Linda? I'm not sure. In a weird way, she doesn't feel important enough to generate a desire for revenge any more. If it hadn't been her, after all, it would have been someone else.

It's impossible, though, to know where our blind spots lie – the 'unknown unknowns', the motivations that lurk outside our conscious awareness. Writing this feels positive rather than destructive, so I am choosing to trust that feeling. Revenge is part of the wolf I want to keep on starvation rations. I don't think it would feel positive.

And I hope you remember the dragons? We haven't talked about them lately, but that doesn't mean they've gone away. I almost see them out of the corner of my eye sometimes, but then I can't be sure whether I'm just seeing a shadow or a trick of the light. I know they are coming. But they are coming in their own time, not mine. There is nothing I can do, I realise. It is not up to me when they appear and disappear. They will come when they are ready.

What do I want from them? What do they want from me? I can worry at this, turn it over and around, tell myself stories about what will happen, what the dragons want, when I will meet them, how I will meet them, what the point of it all might be... I can tangle my mind in endless what ifs...; what if I'm wrong about the dragons? What if they eat me? What if they are angry? What if I faint in terror and miss them? What if they never come and I just end up waiting for them forever? One what if just leads to another and another until there is a huge castle built entirely of what ifs...

So I can tie up my mind in spiralling speculations about things I am powerless to influence right now – or I can just get on with my days and wait for life to unfold. Which would be best for me, do you think?

– 21 –

I HAVE A DARK SIDE...
(CONTINUED)

Lovely Donald attributed all that had happened to his dark side, as if it were a kind of malign entity that possessed him, controlling him almost against his will and removing all empathy or concern for me and his family. His Dark Side was a surgeon, too, performing a 'guiltectomy', a surgical removal of his conscience, so that he could feel no sense of wrongdoing or guilt.

I have a dark side too. Maybe we all do. And I know I said that before, but it is important and bears repeating. None of us is perfect. We all have a dark side.

Once Lovely Donald's dark side had revealed itself in all its refusal to even attempt honesty, I took the leash off my own dark side, removed its muzzle and let it have a run round the garden. It needed to let off steam. It needed to have a good, loud bark and a bit of snarling and growling.

Satan, in the shape of one of my sisters, whispered in my

ear when we went to visit Lovely Donald in the Chapel of Rest at the funeral director's. 'Remember how much Donald hated cucumbers?' she said. 'Well, we need to go to Sainsbury's anyway. We could buy every cucumber they have and work out mathematically how to stuff as many as possible into Donald's coffin. Let him go to his eternal rest mingled with cucumbers...' She was joking, lightening the mood, as we visited my dead husband of thirty-four years and a stranger, a man we never knew at all. But...

My Dark Side poked me in the ribs, got my attention, hissed in my ear, *Do it! Do it!* I was tempted... but resisted. I don't suppose many people are overcome with laughter in the Chapel of Rest. We were. Maybe that's dark enough?

My Dark Side had a good old outing while Lovely Donald was still alive, though. As I said earlier, despite knowing how ill he might be, I did not give him any kind of easy time as I demanded answers, the truth about what had been happening. I didn't hesitate to highlight the many inconsistencies, contradictions and even impossibilities in his various, ever-changing stories. No lie could explain away the text message, and even less so the emails and lies told about me to Friend Dick. Lovely Donald turned and twisted, all his coping strategies deserting him. He suffered. Do you remember what he said at this point? '*You ask questions like a barrister. It's not fair.*'

At one point, I referred to Linda as 'the Fuckbitch' – pretty much an insult to dogs, really, but it was the best my Dark Side could come up with at the time. I saw Donald wince, and assumed he disliked hearing his beloved described in that way. He protested

– but about my use of the word 'fuck'. He disliked swearing and always said I swear too much (I probably do). My Dark Side pointed out that I could continue to call Linda 'the fuckbitch' at every opportunity so that she and I could enjoy watching Donald wince every time. And why not? So I did. We strolled along together, my Dark Side and I, singing, *'Me and my shadow…'*

My Dark Side was sufficiently under control that I continued to visit Donald in hospital, to shop for things he needed, to advocate for him with hospital staff when necessary, to update his friends on his condition, to play endless games of Scrabble with him and, sometimes, to talk about things other than the years of deceit and misdirection. I made a special trip to the supermarket to buy the particular lemonade he asked for. Why? I have no idea, except that I was a Wife Bot, and buffering. I told nobody for six weeks and, as this burden became heavier and heavier to carry, I finally cracked and told my sister (not the cucumber one) when she asked the right question one day. She still visited Donald and was kind to him. At the end of what she probably knew was likely to be her final visit, she hugged him goodbye, with compassion for his suffering. My cucumber sister helped me take Lovely Donald's favourite dog up to the hospital ward so that they could say goodbye to each other on the day before Donald died. We are not completely inhuman. We and Lovely Donald shared a long history.

It was the Dark Side of my Dark Side who considered, for five minutes, contacting Linda's adult children and letting them know the truth about their mother and letting them know, too, that the break-up of their parents' marriage was not, as they seem to have believed, all their father's fault. I could have sent them the texts and emails, and even the naked photos (though I only found these after Donald's death – my Dark Side was back on the lead by then). None of this has anything to do with Linda's children, though – why would I cause them distress? Their father seems to have chosen not to tell them about finding their mother and Lovely Donald *in flagrante* at the family home, and no doubt he has his reasons.

My Dark Side did have a little bit of fun with the naked photos, though. Together we thought of all the things we could do with them – post them online, duplicate them and leaflet Linda's village and so on. Then my cucumber sister, my Dark Side and I looked at the photos together, and we realised a couple of things. They'd obviously been taken a good number of years before Linda met Donald. The non-naked photos in the same envelope were dated, and it was a much older Linda face looking out from them. Also, Linda was not exactly glorying in her body in the naked photos. She looked a bit uncomfortable, a bit shamefaced, a bit embarrassed. Or maybe, as the photos seemed to have been taken in a field, she'd just sat her naked bottom down on an anthill. My Dark Side rather hoped so. We put the photos in the pile destined for the bonfire.

I'm not sure whether it was my Dark Side who pushed me into inappropriate, uncontrollable laughter as I followed Lovely Donald's coffin up the steep hill leading to the church where his funeral service was about to be held. It may simply have been a necessary release of tension as I prepared to face what lay ahead.

I'll tell you what happened, and see what you think. You have to realise that Lovely Donald was no lightweight at the best of times, and his massive fluid retention in the days before his death added considerably to his already great heaviness.

To have pall-bearers carry Lovely Donald's coffin up the hill or into church had been vetoed by the funeral director on health and safety grounds, so he was pushed along on a wheeled bier by four of the funeral director's employees. (I hear Lovely Donald muttering about 'health and safety gone mad…')

I followed, accompanied by Father Andrew, my son's godfather and a long-time friend. He was one of only three people who knew about Lovely Donald's secret life at this point. I hadn't exactly chosen to tell him. Various things he'd said had made me think, mistakenly, that he already knew at least some of it. He didn't – he'd been talking more generally about his perception that Lovely Donald treated me with a lack of consideration at times and was unhappy in our marriage, unhappy in his life. As we unscrambled the misunderstanding, I'd been relieved that someone else knew apart from me and my sisters, and I was comforted by the thought that, as a Catholic priest, Father Andrew understands confidentiality, so wouldn't blab. (And he hasn't.)

As we followed the coffin up the steep, steep hill, we both noticed a couple of things. The pace became slower and more funereal as the four men struggled to push the wheeled bier and its weight up the narrow path. We could see the fabric of their jackets stretching across their shoulders as they strained upwards… there was a sense of huge effort. They were struggling.

Father Andrew and I turned to each other, the same thought having pushed into both our minds at the same moment: *If they can't hold on to that coffin, we're toast!* Breathless with laughter, we imagined the headlines in the local press – MOURNERS CRUSHED BY RUNAWAY COFFIN AS VICAR ROLLS DOWN HILL! We readied ourselves to leap sideways should the worst happen, with complete disregard for my stepsons, following a little way behind us...

Was that my Dark Side at work? I think that it was more likely a release of tension, as I said earlier, but also a shared moment of coming face to face with the absolute ridiculousness of life. As Humphrey Bogart says in *Casablanca*, '*It doesn't take much to see that the troubles of three little people don't amount to a hill of beans in this crazy world...*' What? You don't think the world is crazy? Two words: 'President' and 'Trump'.

My Dark Side was certainly hovering by my left shoulder as I delivered my part of Lovely Donald's eulogy, though. The church was packed with people I know and people I've never met. I suppose Linda could even have been there, though I'd asked her to keep away, or else she may have been represented by members of her family who live fairly locally, as I'd learned. How would I know? My Dark Side surveyed the crowd, and slithered and hissed around me, suggesting I could liven things up by scrapping my script and exploding Lovely Donald's secrets in the faces of the congregation. I didn't. I sent my Dark Side to sit on the naughty step until the service was over. I chose my words carefully and told no lies. I managed to focus on Donald's Doctor Jekyll side, the positive things he did.

My Dark Side hasn't always been so compliant, though. She

swallowed two bottles of wine in a single evening in an attempt to stop thought – though all she achieved was a headache for both of us. She and I have got through quite a lot of gin together, not to mention the Laphroaig… And once again she is going to the naughty step. I am rationing our alcohol, whether my Dark Side likes it or not.

Over and over in recent months, my Dark Side has pushed me towards self-pity, despair and oblivion – or revenge. She is insidious and relentless. *Why should I suffer alone*, she whispers. *Why not make Lollipop Linda and Friend Dick pay for what they did?* Especially now that Lovely Donald has escaped all accountability (unless, of course, he is arguing his case with St Peter at the Pearly Gates even as I write this. I'd like to believe this is happening – but I don't).

Should I listen to my Dark Side and act on her promptings? I remember that these are just words and thoughts and feelings. They are not facts and they are not immutable. They will subside if I wait for them to pass. After all, if I try to wreak whatever damage I can in the lives of Lollipop Linda and Friend Dick, will that help me? Will it make my pain less painful? If I feed the pain, feed the raging wolf, focus my attention on the wrongs done to me, who am I damaging? Lovely Donald has gone to wherever renegade clergy go to after death – or else to nothingness. Friend Dick and Lollipop Linda have done their worst and I do not choose to give them any more power over me. In dwelling on them, what they said, what they did, I harm myself more than I could ever harm anyone else. I took the time to write to them both, calmly but clearly. They know my views on what happened. Let that be enough. Lovely Donald, his women and Friend Dick harmed more people than me by their carelessness of the implications and consequences for others of their actions and choices. I have no power over them, but if I did have the power to damage them, what would be gained by adding more hurt, pain and damage to the hurt, pain and damage already caused?

'*What we dwell on, we become.*'

I allow the pain, rage, humiliation, sadness and sense of loss and waste to have their turn. All that I can achieve by trying to push these feelings away is to make them bounce back at me even more strongly. This wouldn't help me. So let the thoughts and feelings be what they are. And allow them to settle. I point out to my Dark Side that she and I are one being. What harms me will ultimately harm her too. We make a bargain. I will not ignore her or pretend she doesn't exist. She will try to curb her destructiveness. We will communicate*.

And I choose:

'Whatsoever things are true, whatsoever things *are* honest, whatsoever things *are* just, whatsoever things *are* pure, whatsoever things *are* lovely, whatsoever things *are* of good report; if *there be* any virtue, and if *there be* any praise, think on these things.'

And if you don't like the biblical quotes – tough. I take my wisdom from where I can find it. The Bible, Buddha, Native American stories, history, poetry, bird life, sci-fi – anywhere. I'm nothing if not eclectic.

* She still wishes we'd bought the cucumbers, though…

PostScript: *I've just come home after taking my dogs for their teatime walk. We saw a double rainbow, an arc within an arc. The outer arc faded as we watched – we almost missed it. Life always offers random moments of beauty.*

– 22 –

THE DRAGONS ARE COMING...

Here I am again – standing in grassland. I have no idea how I got here. I look around me – I see I am in the middle of a roughly rectangular field, maybe the size of a football pitch. To one side, the land slopes gently upwards. A stream runs along the opposite side, shallow, but flowing noisily over stones. Beyond the two short sides of the field lies open land, hills in the far distance. Above me is a clear blue sky, the colour of an unpolluted ocean. There are no clouds and the sun is climbing – it will be a warm day. I know this place. I feel sure I have been here before. But I can't name it or find the memory it triggers. It is, I realise, a battlefield – how do I know this?

Confusion. Maybe the beginning of fear. Do I have to fight a battle? I am, I realise, standing upright, my right hand raised into the air in what feels like an aggressive rather than a defensive stance. And I am wielding aloft a sword – I see its sharp edge and feel its weight. It fits my hand. As I look, I see it is a thing of beauty, despite its deadliness – silver, shining, intricately engraved along the blade, a gleaming golden hilt... Where on earth did I get this?

I look down. I am wearing armour – my helmet, I realise, restricts my view so I raise my visor, which helps a bit. I am protected from head to foot – a gorget encircles my neck, and epaules guard my shoulders. A cuirass covers my chest and back and my arm harness protects my vulnerable arms. I have gauntlets on my hands, leg harness covering my legs, and foot coverings. Beneath my armour I have chain mail and a padded jacket that will help absorb the shock of any blows as well as protecting my skin from the metal armour. I belong in a museum – or on a medieval battlefield. I'm obviously not in a museum, which leaves me with the scarier option. I practise moving – although the armour is heavy, I can move more easily than I expected.

But no one else is here. How can I be about to fight a battle all alone? Someone must have helped me get all this gear on too – who are they? Where are they?

I turn through a full 360-degree circle. Nothing. No one. Just grass, the sound of the stream, birdsong from the birds overhead... A very calm and peaceful scene. Even a beautiful scene. Not a place for bloodshed.

Yet here I am, equipped for battle, though I don't know who I'm supposed to be fighting or why. And it looks as if they've stood me up, anyway. Can I take off this armour and go home? Well, not without assistance, and I'm not sure where I'm going to find that... Maybe I have to clank home? At least I can lower my arm, which is starting to ache.

But wait… I see something… Over there, a kind of shadow, a solidifying of the air… and over there… And over there… As I look again, shapes seem to be forming all around me, a circle, but they are far away and I can't see them properly. I raise my sword…

The air shivers. Dragon shapes begin to form – all sizes, I see, from the size of a chicken, through what I imagine as the size of a tyrannosaurus rex and up to the size of a house… All colours too – I see reds and golds and greens. A blue and silver dragon and a huge and imposing black dragon. They move slowly towards me, all in step with each other, until I can see some of their faces. All of them are looking at me intently, watching me with solemn expressions…

I shift a little, stand up straighter, stiffen my sword arm as my sword catches the sun. Oddly, I am not afraid. I'm not sure what I feel – maybe watchful, ready for whatever is coming, determined to stand my ground. I flourish my sword, just a little.

The dragons stop moving now but are still looking at me, and I think I can detect a kind of sadness in their eyes. Slowly, all together, they shake their heads… and begin to fade. They are gone. I am alone again. I have the strangest feeling that somehow I have disappointed the dragons, missed something important. Missed, in fact, the whole point of our meeting.

Now what do I do?

– 23 –

'I HAVE A DARK SIDE'
(REVISITED)

Please don't think I have full control over my Dark Side – I hope I didn't give you the wrong impression earlier. The point of a Dark Side is that it is dark, wholly or partially out of my conscious awareness, occult not in the sense of being supernatural or magical, but hidden, secret, not showing any obvious signs. I can know my Dark Side up to a point, but beyond that point there can only be speculation. I have the same human capacity for self-deception as everyone else.

I suspect – but don't know – that my Dark Side might have a hand in the naming of Lovely Donald, Friend Dick and Lollipop Linda. Am I, in the names I choose for them, ridiculing them, diminishing them, and so taking a kind of small revenge? Maybe. There again, while I don't possess that sense of entitlement that Lovely Donald and Friend Dick seemed to share, I do feel that I am allowed to derive what amusement I can from this situation, use whatever coping strategy can help me to live with the pain of it. Perhaps if I were truly seeking revenge I'd use their real names in full, no disguises.

The names express something of my experience, my truth – different, obviously from the truth as they perceive it. Perhaps I am choosing names that diminish them not so much from a desire for revenge as from a need to reduce the size and scale of their impact in my life, to make it more manageable. Don't forget that for up to fifteen years Linda and Dick had a huge impact upon my life. I felt the ripples of their behaviour but knew nothing of their influence on Lovely Donald and, through him, on me and my son. Don't forget that everything that happened was happening without my knowledge or consent. I think I am being quite kind in disguising their identities.

Counsellors talk about breaking problems down into bite-sized chunks, so that you do not become overwhelmed by them. It might sound like a cannibalistic metaphor, but I think I'm breaking Lovely Donald et al down into bite-sized chunks.

Q: How do you eat an elephant?
A: One mouthful at a time.

More seriously, perhaps, as I reflect on my life as a whole, I realise that it was probably my Dark Side that got me into this situation in the first place. Like Lollipop Linda, I rescued Lovely Donald when we first met. And how seductive it is, how flattering, to be able to save someone, to be a rescuer. Like Linda, I was the female equivalent of a knight in shining armour, riding along on a beautiful horse, ready to save the day. Had I been even more like Linda, and ready to embark on a long-term secret affair with Donald, willing to visit him clandestinely in his vicarage when his wife was safely absent, then maybe none of this would have happened. I can drive, too, which would, no doubt, have made Donald's life a bit easier. Lovely Donald would still be married to his first wife, perhaps (though I doubt it). I would have tired of being *the other woman* and moved on years ago. Lovely Donald would have replaced me, as dating sites for married people came into being, and at some point his wife would have learned the truth and saved herself. I hope it wouldn't have taken her thirty-four years.

We are in the realm of counter-factual history now. It didn't happen that way. But isn't it interesting to speculate about what might have been? I have said already that I am not innocent. I'm not.

I first met Lovely Donald some thirty-six years ago, partly through work and partly because we had friends in common. With hindsight – good old hindsight galloping in when it is too late to be of any use – I think I inadvertently gave Lovely Donald the wrong idea about who I was, what kind of person I was, though I was unaware of this at the time.

I was – how to put this? – a bit of a mess as I approached my very early thirties. And it's only fair that I tell you my darker secrets, having spent the last 46,267 words telling you about Lovely Donald's.

To Be Continued...

A FULL STOP...

Is what I've come to. I began the previous chapter, intending to continue to the end – I know what I want to say. But visitors arrived, my phone rang – life, in other words, intervened. And since then I've been busy, sorting out more of Lovely Donald's various messes – he was such a hoarder! – and clearing up the messy aftermath of Lovely Donald's life. People have helped me. It would take too much time and too many words to list all the people who have helped me over these last few years. The Helpers.

I have to say, though, that I am tired beyond describing. Partly the consequence of my illness, partly the consequence of the shocks and traumas during these years, partly – I don't know what. Maybe I'm just wearing out, like the shoes I threw away a couple of days ago because they were no longer fit for purpose.

My son's absence is the central fact I face in every waking minute of every day. Within that, though, some days are easier than others. Some days are harder.

Early mornings are the worst. Murf would often phone or text me early in the morning, around 7 a.m. He knew I'd be in my conservatory, drinking my coffee, a dog on my knee, a book in my hand. Often we'd talk about nothing in particular; sometimes *we'd talk about something. It varied. We'd talk.*

Now I don't know which is hardest to bear – hearing my phone remain steadfastly silent, or hearing its ringtone or message alert and knowing that it is not my son who is calling. It is never my son who is calling.

I live in a perpetual present now. Murf's death stole my future. All the young people around me remind me that a future exists – perhaps. Though not for my son and not for me.

The past is lost to me. Lovely Donald and his various Lindas stole much of my past, my memories. All I know of my life with Lovely Donald rests on quicksand, no solid ground. It is wreathed with mists that confuse the eye. There are no reliable landmarks or road maps for this territory that lies beyond the known world. There is little point in visiting; I cannot trust what I see. There are other memories, of course, of other parts of my life, but Lovely Donald is threaded through all of the last thirty-four years. In this treacherous landscape, he was busily turning all the signposts round to send me in wrong directions, deliberately putting me and his family in harm's way.

So I have only this moment, now – and this is true, of course, for all of us in every moment. This present moment, right now, isn't much fun, though. I'm sick, beyond my powers to describe, of effort, making an effort to move through each leaden, draining day – day by day, one day at a time, one foot in front of the other, keeping calm and carrying on. I know that the journey of a thousand miles starts with a single step, but sometimes even that single step can feel overwhelming – and then there are all the other steps, waiting their turn.

Humour rarely deserts me, the ability to find a kind of joy in small things rarely deserts me – but today they have both gone walkabout. I guess they are off somewhere, having fun together, needing a break from the omnipresence of Grief.

I awoke this morning to a damp, grey sky outside my window and a damp, grey despair in every cell of my body. Everything hurts. It is hard, because painful, to move. But move I must – if only because the dogs still have to be walked. And for myself, too, I must move.

My son's ex-girlfriend came for tea last night. As I sat opposite her at the kitchen table, my mind travelled easily down the road of What if's and If only's. If only she and Murf had stayed together, he'd never have met Natalya and everything would have been different... Pointless, futile circles.

I'm fond of this young woman. She lived with us for a time, and she is, I think, the only person whose grief for my son is as all-pervasive as mine. She also has her own sense of betrayal at the gap between the Lovely Donald she thought she knew and the Lovely Donald who emerged in those last few months. I want her to have a fulfilled life, but I know how my son's non-existence in the world overshadows everything for her, as it does for me. I took her home after we'd eaten and then felt too tired to wash up.

Tackling the dirty pots this morning, I noticed two of my very sharp Sabatier kitchen knives lurking seductively on the drainer. I didn't touch them. I looked at them. How easy it would be to open a vein or an artery and let my life escape. Just let go of effort. Bleed visibly as well as invisibly. I begin to understand more clearly the release described by people who cut themselves, the sense of tension flowing out with the blood.

I considered the logistics – I know which way to cut my arm to achieve death, leaving the doors unlocked so the emergency services can gain entry. Calling them at the right moment – too soon and they will save me. Too late and I will be unable to make the call. I wouldn't want anyone else to find me... The bathroom would be the best place – easiest to clean and I could close the door to keep out the dogs... I trace the practical steps in my mind...

The dogs. Both of them are sitting in the kitchen, heads on one side in that way terriers have, watching me closely. Do they know what is in my mind?

Responsibility comes to my rescue, if rescue is what it is. The dogs need their walk. It is my mother's birthday in a few days. I need to pay the decorator, the solicitor, the stonemason who is making Lovely Donald's memorial stone...

Is the image of someone – anyone – finding me dead in a bath full of blood really the legacy I want to leave to all these people, young and old, who have cared for me and supported me? One of my niblings*, in the aftermath of my son's death, was motivated to begin to train as a mental health first-aider at work. 'We can do nothing,' she said, 'to change this horrible thing that has happened. At least if, through this experience, I'm able to help somebody else, then something positive will come from it.' This heartened me. Recently she sent me a photo of a note somebody had left in a wood near to her home, where recently several people have taken their own lives. It read, 'Suicide doesn't end the pain. It just passes it on to someone else.' I put the knives, and the thoughts, in the knife block.

Despair is a heavy old wolf, grey and weary, plodding along arthritically by my side. It would like to savage me, but lacks the energy now – and anyway, it needs me. It? Despair is a living, breathing creature. He, then. He needs me. I feed him and keep him company in the moments when we are both completely alone except for each other. He is not my friend, but he is my familiar companion. He is reluctant to leave today. We're stuck with each other. He is a shapeshifter, this wolf Despair. Sometimes he seems to be the size of a chihuahua, and at other times, like today, he is bigger than any wolf that ever hunted in a forest.

But this will pass. Despair will move on for a time, seeking companionship elsewhere. Humour will return from her truancy and help with the washing up.

There is always something positive in my immediate experience if I can manage to seek it out – hard to do when Despair is filling up my vision. I remember the prayer of St Teresa of Avila that I had pinned up on my kitchen wall for years: 'Let nothing disturb you, nothing make you afraid. All things are passing…'

Despair has plodded on a little ahead of me now. Maybe he won't notice that I've fallen behind? I'll move a little more slowly, let him get further ahead for now. We'll catch up with each other, I know, but it is good to have some time apart. He sneaked into the car and came with me and the dogs to the lake, but he lay down under a tree and went to sleep, despite the rain. We tiptoed away. He hasn't come home with us.

*My word of the week is 'niblings', a word I learned only recently. It is the collective noun for one's nieces and nephews – niblings.

Like 'mamaguy', it makes me smile, but without the deceptiveness of 'mamaguy'. I think about my niblings and great-niblings. I wonder why we have 'grand' children, but 'great' nieces and nephews?

− 24 −

SEPTEMBER: MEMORIES

This was going to be a return to my Dark Side – well, we have to come back to it eventually, don't we? I've had a few days of unwellness and a general can't-be-bothered-ness, a lethargy, but today's a new day. Maybe I've just been unwell – I think that's true – but I recall that September is a month of anniversaries. Anniversaries, it occurs to me, can be difficult. Whether positive or negative, they stir up past and present emotions. I am reliving past events in my mind's eye and in my gut – much more the seat of emotion than the heart for me. It would be unsurprising if my emotional state reflected itself in my physical being.

Seeing all the children going back to school became time travelling. It took me in an instant to all my son's first days back at school. Watching the mothers taking their children to school reminded me that I am no longer a mother. It's strange, isn't it, that there isn't a word for a mother whose child has died? If your husband dies, you become a widow. A child whose parents die is an orphan. What do you become when your only child dies? An ex-mother? There isn't a word. There ought to be. It is a state of being that needs a name. I never know, now, what to say when a stranger asks me if I have children, grandchildren. If I say I don't, that feels like denying my son's existence. If I say that I had a son but he died, that makes the asker feel uncomfortable and can involve an awkward conversation. If someone asks me if I'm married, I can just say that I am a widow and that's enough. I can't think of a suitable name for a bereaved mother, though. Any suggestions? Remember, it needs to be a word that is self-explanatory, because an invented word whose meaning has to be explained to most people just takes me right back to where I began, having to give an explanation.

Don't forget that September is a month of anniversaries. I remember the time when my son would have been about eight, I think, and we had a serendipitous day off. We turned up at school on the first day of the autumn term to find the gates locked, the building dark and deserted. The only people around were half a dozen other parents with their children, all of us locked out together. It was a small school, but it was obvious that there must be at least 100 or so people, not including teachers, who knew something we didn't.

One of the dads, who lived nearby, went home to make some phone calls. He came back twenty minutes later. There had been a letter telling parents that the start of term had been postponed by twenty-four hours. He'd managed to speak to the head teacher, and she'd managed to work out that our children were the ones who had been absent from school on the day the letters were given out… Oh dear.

Now this was a problem for those parents who'd expected to drop off their children and go to work, but, fortuitously, they all had solutions in mind. I didn't even have a problem to solve – I was not due to work that day, anyway. My son and I decided it would be too much of an anticlimax to just go home, so we went off to the Science Museum, had a lovely day and a nice lunch, and went home in time for tea. This is a happy memory. I'm not sure who was more pleased by the unexpected holiday, me or my son, but together we made the most of it. Happy days!

There are other memories too. In September 2017, a month before the Shattering, Lovely Donald and I were on our way to South Wales for what I think we both suspected might be his last holiday. We were taking the dogs and going to a cottage for three weeks. It was okay. Lovely Donald wasn't well, to the point where I suggested we seek medical advice. He refused, and seemed a little better as the days went by. We pottered – walked the dogs on those beaches of the Gower Peninsula that are dog-friendly, went for lunch, had fish and chips and ice cream, did a few short walks on the coastal path, visited a few places of historical interest. Lovely Donald was quiet, slept quite a lot, but seemed to be enjoying himself. I read books. He watched TV. I helped him with the *Guardian* crossword. I wonder what he'd have made of 6 across in the crossword I did today – '*A dupe in Slavic times? (6 letters)*' Lovely Donald helped me with Sudoku.

It was his seventieth birthday while we were away – he had timed it deliberately so that we would be away on his birthday. He didn't want a fuss, he said. He was happy to reach threescore years and ten – the lifespan allotted to humanity in the Bible – and said that the time to celebrate would be when he reached eighty. Neither of us seriously believed this was likely to happen, but we pretended to believe it and planned what we might do for his eightieth birthday party in 2027. We watched a DVD of *I, Daniel Blake* together. We both cried. We appeared to have the same response to the lack of humanity in our present political and economic system. We talked about the politics of austerity. I was probably intellectually challenging, but he seemed to enjoy the conversations, to be engaged.

The week before his birthday, Lovely Donald insisted on going to Glastonbury for the day. Glastonbury was one of his favourite places and we had been there many times, with our son, with other family members and often just the two of us. Apparently he never went there with Lollipop Linda, though that might have been more her doing than his. Did he go with his other women? No idea.

I was unsure about the wisdom of going – it was a long drive and a wet day – poor driving conditions. Lovely Donald was adamant. I think now that he thought it might be the last time he would go there. It was.

We separated. He wandered round the High Street a bit and I went into the Speaking Tree – isn't that a lovely name for a bookshop? I think we might have had a meal in the Blue Note Café or the George and Pilgrims, or did we buy sandwiches at Burns the Bread? I can't remember. Lovely Donald found a picture he liked. It cost £70. This seemed like a sign, he said, so I bought it for his birthday. I still have it, hanging on my wall.

Donald wanted to climb up the Tor – again I was unsure he was well enough. He was going to climb up it with or without me, though, so I opted to go with him. We took a dog each. Lovely Donald has usually been better at the climb than me, but this time it was easy for me to be far ahead of him. He didn't want me to wait for him – 'I'm better left to get on with it myself,' he said. I'd have felt the same, so did as he asked.

Eventually, he and the bigger dog (Donald's favourite) joined me and the little dog at the top. It was cold, wet and windy so we didn't stay long. Lovely Donald said goodbye to the St Michael Tower, the place, the view. He reminded me that he wanted me to scatter his ashes up here – 'You're assuming you will die first,' I said. There is an intimacy in that situation, that conversation, that is hard to fathom now, when all memories are tainted by what came later. Lovely Donald had so little regard for me and yet, in the end, he had no one else he could trust to make sure his last wishes were respected. None of his women, Lollipop Linda included, were there when he needed them. I wonder if he thought about any of this? It feels desperately sad.

We agreed that I would go down first, put the little dog in the car, and then return for the bigger dog – my issues with balance made it perilous for me to try to walk downhill with both dogs. Lovely Donald would make his way down slowly and see how far he could get before I returned.

Not very far, it appeared. When I returned, I could see he was struggling. I called to him to let go of the dog, and I rattled a handful of dog treats – I knew my greedy Border terrier would head straight for the sound. And – predictably – he did. So I took him to the car, left him with the little dog.

Back I went for Lovely Donald. It was getting quite late in the afternoon by this time – still cold, still wet, still windy. Lovely Donald walked a few steps, sat down if there was a bench to sit on or stood still for a while, and then walked a few more steps. He shouted to me to let him make his own way down, and, in truth, there was little I could do to help him.

At this point I became aware of one of those anonymous helpers who appear in my life from time to time. There was a young, active-looking woman walking behind Lovely Donald. She struck me as someone who could have run down that hill very easily, but she was walking at his pace, stopping when he stopped. She noticed me looking at her and waved to me, gesturing towards Lovely Donald. She was making sure he got down the hill safely, ready to help him should he need help, ready to help me should I need help to get him back to the car. My heart lifted as I understood what she was doing.

And Lovely Donald made it back to the bottom of the hill under his own steam – we both noted this as an achievement. The dark-haired young guardian angel ran past, waving as she went, her wings tucked safely out of the rain. I waved back, with gratitude for her kindness. Sometimes, only kindness matters.

It was just a short walk to the car. We went for a coffee. Lovely Donald seemed to revive. Did he know he was about to leave Glastonbury for the last time?

Had he died there, on Glastonbury Tor, I think that would have been something he'd have been grateful for. He'd have liked to die there, I think, in a place that meant something to him. Had he died on the Tor that cold, wet day, it would have been a fitting end. I would have mourned him genuinely and sincerely, as would everyone who knew him or believed they knew him. I would still have learned about his affairs, his lies and his relationship with Lollipop Linda because of the little IEDs he'd left in various parts of our home, but he would have died believing his secrets to be safe. He would have died without that horrible last four months when I tried to reconcile the person I'd thought I knew with the person now in front of me. I think I wish it had happened that way – it would have been kinder, somehow.

A friend said that he got what he deserved at the end, with his realisation that his secrets were no longer secret, his watertight compartments truly breached. He knew I thought less of him and others would think less of him. I think, on balance, I'd have preferred to spare him that knowledge had it been possible to do so. I am still mindful of the abandoned baby, the bereaved child in a house filled with loss, and really, at this late stage, what good was done by confronting him? He did nothing but lie – and perhaps, so many years on from the first lie, there was nothing else he could do. Friend Dick, in a rare moment that sounded like insight, said that after all the years of lying, Lovely Donald no longer knew how to do anything but lie. As I type that, I have to stop, breathe, absorb the impact of that thought.

So I think I would have liked Donald to go gently into death on the top of Glastonbury Tor, remembering the view obscured that day by the greyness of the rain and the clouds, letting go of life in St Michael Tower with his favourite dog beside him.

That's not an unselfish thought. Such an end for him might have spared me something too. If he had died that day, once I'd found the letters, photos and the rest of it, I would never have known whether he might, at the end, have told the truth, have been honest with me. I think it would have been an easier journey for me if that could have remained a possibility – that he might have felt guilt, remorse or at least some regret for the harm done. I'd like to have been able to believe that might have happened. There is something deadening, even frightening, in knowing that he felt none of that, expressed none of that, but could only describe his sense that he was entitled to do all he did, to have his secrets, his 'bit of excitement'. The coldness he showed in these conversations left me – I'm not sure where it left me. In a strange place of darkness, and some fear, perhaps. Sometimes it is possible that certainty is more painful than uncertainty, because uncertainty contains possibility. Certainty removes possibility. Schrodinger's cat pops into my mind, both dead and alive until you open the box. Lovely Donald might have wanted to explain, apologise, might have cared something about me in another world that doesn't exist. His survival beyond that day in Glastonbury removed all doubt, all possibility, all hope. It opened the box.

September 2017 was the last month in which I could believe I had a marriage of sorts. Now that time has passed, what I feel is sadness, a sense of loss. I've asked myself how I grieve for Lovely Donald, my husband of thirty-four years, and a man I never knew, never truly met until the end of his life. I grieve for lost possibilities, for the Donald he might have been, and appeared to be. I cannot rid myself of the thought that at some level, deep inside himself, he wanted to be the Donald we thought we knew – flawed as we all are, but possessing integrity and true concern for others. He just didn't know how to be in fact the person he pretended to be. I grieve for myself, my state of unknowing, for what might be seen, in some lights, as my wasted life. I don't grieve for Donald's death, but I do grieve for how he lived his life. I grieve for the impact on his children of the choices he made. I grieve for everyone who now has to think again about how they knew who Lovely Donald was, and has to deal with their own sense of betrayal. Lovely Donald left many complexities for others to unravel as best they can, and I grieve for the impact of that carelessness. I have said before that he didn't age well; be sure your sin will find you out. I could see the corrosion in his face, his soul, even before I knew what it was. I grieve that he had to live with that corrosion, the consequence of choices made. That he died with it.

The holiday, taken as a whole, was – all right. Quiet. I continued to be concerned about Lovely Donald's physical state. He continued to disregard my concerns. I felt at the time that there was something elegiac about his mood – particularly one day when he sat on a headland looking out to sea whilst I walked the dogs on the beach below. Maybe I imagined it, that sadness, that regret. The day of his seventieth birthday was a day of downpours and real cold that cut through coats and waterproofs. Even the dogs wanted to stay in. Donald had wanted to go for lunch to a particular pub we'd seen as we'd driven around. When we got there, it was closed for renovations.

And I don't have to listen to the promptings of my Dark Side now that I know what I know. I will dispose of Lovely Donald's ashes as he wished. It seems like the least I can do. I am doing it for him in part, but mostly I am doing it for myself. What kind of person would I be if I did anything other than respect his wishes now?

And none of this is what I set out to write in this chapter. Sometimes, as I write, the words seem to take on a life of their own. I may have said something about this before. They insist on being set down in their way, which is not always the way I have planned or intended. It feels better to go with the flow of the words, though – I feel that they need to come as they want to come and that there is a reason for this, even though I may not understand that reason on any conscious level. And if you are thinking that I should be more disciplined, impose a greater degree of structure, or that I am writing drivel, then you could be right, I suppose. But I'm writing what I'm writing.

I'm not avoiding talking about how my Dark Side led me to Lovely Donald. That was what I had intended to write about here. But as I've journeyed into September, watched the children walking past my window to the school round the corner, realised I don't need to buy Lovely Donald a birthday present, reflected on my son's schooldays, I've recognised that some of my unwellness, my exhaustion, my sadness derives from the emotion of this month of anniversaries and my memories of that last September holiday. Best to face these things, acknowledge them, examine them. Was it Socrates who said that the unexamined life is not worth living? I cannot help thinking that if Lovely Donald had examined his life more thoroughly, he would have lived it differently. My Dark Side will still be there tomorrow; it can wait. We'll get to it next time.

It's a lovely evening after a day of showers. In a minute, I will walk the dogs. On this evening in 2017, Donald and I, in a companionable moment, were walking the dogs on a beach in South Wales, enjoying the late afternoon sunshine, enjoying watching the dogs' uncomplicated pleasure in the freedom of sea and sand. We laughed, I think I remember, at the little dog's cautious approach to the waves, the bigger dog's love of splashing chest-deep in the water, both living so completely in the moment. Happy days?

− 25 −

BACK TO THE DARK SIDE − FINALLY

Q: What lies on the bottom of the sea and shivers?
A: A nervous wreck.

Wreck: something... that has been badly damaged or destroyed
O.E.D.

As I've thought about this chapter, there has been a nigglingly persistent image in my mind. It's me in an old-fashioned diving suit, with the weighted shoes, lead belt and big, round diving helmet. But I'm going wreck-diving, and the beautiful old diving suit, with its brass fittings, but also with its umbilical cord reaching up to the boat – well, it's just not suitable, is it?

So – reluctantly – I banish that image. I'm wearing a wet suit – bright orange, unforgiving. I'm not overweight, but I'm not the right shape for a wetsuit, especially a bright orange one. It's got a turquoise stripe across it – hideous. But I'm going wreck-diving, not entering a fashion show. *Just get on with it and stop moaning*, I tell myself. Wreck-diving is a dangerous enterprise, and I'm lucky to have all this state-of-the-art scuba-diving gear, even if it does mean I have to wear an orange and turquoise wetsuit. I'm in deep waters here and I need all the help I can get.

SS *Lovely Donald* is down there in the darkness, somewhere, at the bottom of the sea. It's more than possible that I might find the wreck of SS *Hoodwinked Hattie* too, though she's not marked on the charts for this area. This is a hazardous stretch of water, akin to the Pentland Firth. There are hidden rocks, perilous to shipping, and the strength and speed of the tides creates whirlpools and races. It's a scary place for mariners, and even the most skilful ship's captain might come to grief here. There are even stories of wreckers using false lights from the cliffs to lure storm-tossed vessels to their doom, readying them for plunder. There are many dead ships under this water and not all of them are marked on the charts. Few people survive shipwreck here; mostly the sea takes them, and there are dark tales that years ago the wreckers murdered those few who did manage to struggle to the shore. SS *Friend Dick* and SS *Lollipop Linda* do not lie in these waters: they continue afloat, sailing the high seas. Their crews ignored the distress flares and Mayday signals from SS *Lovely Donald* – they had better things to do than try to help a ship that was probably already beyond saving. Maybe, like the crew of the *Californian* who ignored the distress flares from the *Titanic*, they had turned off their radio for the night and thought the flares were a firework display. They never even noticed the SS *Hoodwinked Hattie*'s distress flares; they were too intent on their own journeys and that insignificant little ship meant nothing to them. Let her sink or not – she must take her chances.

I am seeking understanding of the years of my life. How could Lovely Donald treat me, and his children, as he did? How could he create such a powerful and mostly convincing persona of a caring, sensitive man of integrity and faith while simultaneously betraying his marriage, his family and his ordination vows? Not to mention the senior clergy who enabled him to return to ministry five years after he left his first wife? How could he spend so many years in lies? I realise that many of my questions will never have answers: Lovely Donald has passed beyond accountability for his actions and choices. But I have to live with the consequences, and I look to the past so I can try to piece together what can be known. Hence my explorations in these dark, dangerous waters.

I said I am going wreck-diving, but I am beginning to question that now. Good old Wikipedia tells me that wreck-diving is '... *recreational diving where the wreckage of ships, aircraft and other artificial structures are explored... some wreck-diving involves penetration of the wreckage, making a direct ascent to the surface impossible for a part of the dive...*' In other words, there are risks attached to wreck-diving. The diver may get lost or trapped in the wreck and run out of oxygen – and die.

But what I am doing is not recreational, not something I am doing for interest or pleasure. I am exploring the wreckage of my life in order to make it as safe as possible, to let the past be the past, to accommodate it, without being damaged beyond all possibility of survival.

So maybe this is underwater archaeology, then. Turning to Wikipedia once more I learn that underwater archaeology '...*now has a number of branches including, after it became broadly accepted in the late 1980s, maritime archaeology: the scientifically based study of past human life, behaviours and cultures and their activities on, around and under the sea, estuaries and rivers.*' Well, I'm not sure how scientifically based my endeavours might be, but this sounds more like it. It's still dangerous; a diver can still get lost or trapped, but I'm doing this in pursuit of understanding and truth, not for fun.

When I was training to be a counsellor, possibly around the time Lovely Donald began exploring internet dating for married people, water was often used as a metaphor for the emotions. Do you prefer to stay in the shallows, never doing more than paddling, or do you feel able to swim out of your depth? Allow the water to support you? Take a few risks?

If I roll up my trouser legs, take off my shoes and socks and just dip my toes in the water, I can stay safe in the shallows. Lovely Donald was a liar and a cheat who deceived me and abused my trust. He let his children down in a variety of ways without compunction. He chose to associate with like-minded people – Lollipop Linda, Friend Dick – when the strain of pretending virtues he did not possess became too much. I was, and am, an innocent victim, the 'dupe in Slavic times'.

That's one version of the truth, albeit one that simplifies complexities. I cannot give you Lovely Donald's version, because, in the end, he never offered one, beyond saying that he had a dark side and was 'crap' at close relationships.

Maybe I need to swim a little further out, though, and look at what I have contributed to the wreckage. Disasters rarely have single causes; often a perfect storm of what might individually be quite small factors comes together in a particular constellation that, ultimately, makes the disaster unavoidable. The iceberg and the *Titanic*. Lovely Donald and the exposure of his secret life. Me and Lovely Donald. My son and Death.

I told you a while back that I first met Lovely Donald when I was thirty or thirty-one, at a time in my life when I was not at my best. Just to recap, '*I was – how to put this? – a bit of a mess as I approached my very early thirties.*'

Like Lollipop Linda, I had married too soon, aged twenty, to a man who was a decent enough human being (as I think I am too), but with whom, in the end, I was not compatible. We were married for just over ten years – happily enough to begin with, but I suppose I became dissatisfied, restless, unfulfilled. I was working long hours in a busy and stressful job, and as I approached thirty, realised that I wanted children. My husband and I had little in common, really, and a major difference between us was that he was very clear that he did not want children and did not believe that he would ever change his mind. He had his reasons; they seemed good to him, but less so to me.

So many years have passed since that time – I can barely remember what it felt like to be the person I was back then. As

I think about myself and all that happened, I could almost be thinking about a stranger. I scarcely recognise my younger self. As I swim through the wrecks, it is hard to see, hard to find any reference points.

Let's be honest here – I did not behave well. I did not treat my husband well. I did try to discuss my discontent with him and explore our differences; he felt I was making a fuss about nothing. We were fine. I thought too much, he said. I'd get over the wish for children – after all, I hadn't wanted children when I was in my twenties, training, establishing my career. As I expressed concerns, he busily brushed them away as *blips*, niggles, nothing important. I wondered if perhaps he was right; but then I knew he wasn't, at least, not for me.

I drifted into an affair with a work colleague, a man I knew to be married but also knew to have had multiple brief affairs with many women. Let's call him Tony, though that wasn't his name. When I think back to that time, I have absolutely no idea what led me into this affair with a man in whom I had no real interest and who, if the truth be told, I didn't even like very much. I also – maybe I'm old-fashioned – felt that it was wrong to have an affair with a married man, even as I was doing that very thing. It's possible that I was avoiding issues, unconsciously looking for a way to end my marriage, using Tony to help me make the break – who knows? But this was not an honest or even an intelligent way to deal with my problems in my relationship with my husband; how on earth could having an affair help?

I can't even say that I was flattered by Tony's attention and interest in me. I remember knowing, even then, that there was nothing flattering about being paid attention by Tony. He paid attention to every woman he met; he had affairs with a fair few of them.

I soon learned that I'm not good at secrecy and deception. I don't enjoy them; they make me twitchy. I lied to my husband, family and friends at times because, obviously, I did not want them to know what I was doing. But I hated it – hated lying, and disliked myself for doing it. In the end I couldn't sustain it, and told my husband and my family about Tony. Questions: what did I think I was doing? Were Tony and I going to end our marriages and set up home together? And even the thought of that made me shiver with horror.

Another source of discomfort for me was that I'd learned, through a fairly weird set of coincidences, that I'd actually been to primary school with Tony's wife. We'd gone to different schools aged eleven, and I'd never seen her again, but nonetheless I'd known her. I don't know why this should have made a difference, but it did. Somehow she became, in my mind, not just Tony's anonymous wife, whom I'd never met, but a real person with feelings. What I was doing was unfair to her too, whether she knew about it or not.

It was all fairly messy and painful. My husband wanted us to put the affair behind us and stay together. I realised that I didn't want this, and eventually I left and moved into a fairly grotty flat close to where I worked. The affair with Tony ended, and he found another job – a promotion – 200 miles away. We didn't keep in touch. I heard, via a mutual acquaintance a few years later, that he was now working his way through a whole new set of women in his new job. 'Leopards and spots,' said my acquaintance. I should have paid more attention.

Lovely Donald was a friend of Tony's – maybe this should have put me on my guard, but it didn't. I think that I was, naively, reassured that he was 'safe' by his dog collar. I can't believe I could have thought that – but I did. I can't believe that I was that stupid – but I was.

Like me, Lovely Donald was part of a group of people, all working in caring roles, who used to meet up for lunch once or twice a week, work allowing. It was a fluid group. We'd plan to meet on Wednesday, for example, and it wasn't uncommon for one or more people to have to cancel at the last minute because of some sort of crisis at work. I confided in Lovely Donald a little bit – he was very easy to talk to. I think I inadvertently misled him into thinking I was someone who would have affairs with married men, because, after all, I'd put myself into that category through my relationship with Tony. And by this time I was living apart from my husband. My Dark Side had been pretty busy.

However, the end of my marriage and the affair with Tony had taught me a few things – including the fact that adultery was not for me. I couldn't cope with the dishonesty, the necessary secrecy nor with the sense of wrongdoing, the betrayal of another woman, whether I knew her or not. I'd learned, too, that I'd treated my husband unfairly. In future, I'd decided, I'd only get involved with single men and if a relationship was not working, I'd end it before beginning another. Any other way involves too much hurt and pain for too many people – including me. Good intentions…

I did discuss this a little bit with Lovely Donald, I think, but maybe I didn't, or maybe he didn't believe me. Again, who knows?

By this time, Lovely Donald and I were having lunch together, just the two of us. I wasn't wise enough at this point to understand that affairs can take more than one form; they aren't always sexual. I was allowing an inappropriate emotional closeness to develop between me and Lovely Donald, and I was foolish and short-sighted enough to believe that this was innocent. My Dark Side was being a bit more subtle, a bit more clever this time. Maybe Lovely Donald believed this was innocent too. Maybe he believed I'd embark on a physical affair with him, if only to cheer him up. I have no idea what he thought. What's the point in speculating? Whatever was going on with my Dark Side or his Dark Side, in talking to me, building closeness with me, he was removing energy from his marriage. He was not talking to his wife. At first I thought we were helping each other; I listened to my Dark Side as she whispered in my ear.

Fairly quickly, though, the balance changed, and rather than me confiding in Lovely Donald, he was confiding in me. I am not going to repeat what he told me about Vicky, his first wife, because I know now that there was little, if any, truth in any of it. She was not and is not the person he represented her to be – someone eerily similar, in fact, to the person he later represented me to be when talking to Friend Dick and unknown others. I don't believe that I am that person either, but maybe both Vicky and I became that person in his eyes, in his experience and projections?

The more Lovely Donald confided in me, the more concerned I became about his mental state. He talked of drinking a bottle of sherry most nights. He'd been to a massage parlour for 'hand relief' and was consumed by guilt, self-loathing and a sense of being unclean. He talked of the suicide rate in clergy... (I actually have no idea whether the suicide rate is higher among the clergy than in other occupational groups. I didn't check. I trusted Lovely Donald.) He was, he said, more than 'half in love with easeful death'; sometimes it seemed like the only way out. His children, then quite young, would be better off with one parent than living in a war zone...

And the balance changed again. I could save him. We could make a fresh start, he could continue to support his children without subjecting them to living with endless conflict... I wasn't sure this was a good idea. Maybe he owed it to his family to try to make it work? Maybe he should talk to a doctor or a marriage guidance counsellor rather than to me?

But no, he said. The damage was too great. The only hope was for him to leave. This would, of course, mean he had to leave the church, but he might be able to go back one day and in the meantime, he could return to his original job in the public sector. Vicky deserved honesty. He owed it to her, in fact, to leave. As I type all this, it sounds wholly unconvincing. What can I say? It sounded convincing at the time. Maybe, too, as that Irish comedian – what was his name? – used to say, 'It's the way I tell 'em...'

Let's cut to the chase. As I said before, few things are more seductive than believing that you can save someone. I smothered my doubts, my sense of wrongdoing in the egotism of being a rescuer – I told you that I have a Dark Side. Lovely Donald moved in with me and before long I was pregnant. We seemed to be making a life together. We seemed happy. He seemed happy. He seemed to be continuing to be a caring father to his two children, difficult as Vicky made that at times, (he said). He thought it was best if I kept out of his relationship with his children as much as possible; my involvement would only make things even trickier with Vicky. I believed him. Of course, this also meant that I saw little of the children, never had a conversation with Vicky... right up to the time of the elder boy's marriage, more than twenty years later. It would be best I didn't go to the reception, said Lovely Donald. We didn't want my presence to spoil Vicky's day. (In fact, my presence wouldn't have made any difference to Vicky's enjoyment of the day, but I still believed Lovely Donald's version – probably because he believed it himself.) We all stayed in the watertight compartments Lovely Donald had constructed for us. This meant, of course, that we never compared notes.

And that brings me back to the slipperiness of truth. I know I've asked this question several times now, but it bears repeating. Whose truth is true?

As I recount this history, I reflect on the notorious unreliability of eyewitness testimony. I am telling you my experience, what I believed to be true – but Lovely Donald, Vicky, her children, my ex-husband, even Tony and his wife – they all had their own versions of the truth too. Telling a story, a history, involves selection and interpretation and relies on memory, which is all too fallible. I am making judgements about what happened, always dangerous – like wreck-diving and marine archaeology. You can take a wrong turn, get stuck in a corner, run out of oxygen. History is selective and we can never really know with certainty exactly what happened and exactly how it felt for everyone involved. Moment by moment we create our own world through the choices we make and where we focus our attention. We tell ourselves stories about our lives and though these stories may become distorted by time and the unreliability of memory, the stories are seen as truths.

So maybe I'm wasting my time and yours, down here in the murky and turbulent waters. What happened, happened. It was what it was. It is the past. It is history. Whatever happened, it can't be changed now. There are few answers.

I can go back to the surface and take off this bloody wetsuit. I'm about to turn to clichés again: I heard something like this float out of Radio Four when I turned the car radio on one day, while waiting for my son outside school:

The past is history,
The future – a mystery.
This moment – now – is a gift,
Which is why it's called the present.

Trite perhaps, but I've remembered it all these years. L. P. Hartley put it better in the opening sentence of *The Go-*

Between: '*The past is a foreign country; they do things differently there.*' As my son used to say irritatingly often, 'We are where we are.' And I am here. Now.

– 26 –

I'LL GET IT RIGHT THIS TIME – I'M GOING TO MEET THE DRAGONS

Five minutes, that's all. I just closed my eyes for five minutes. Lovely Donald was a hoarder, and it has taken much of my time and more of my precious energy to bring some order to his room, my house and the shed. My nieces and I filled a maxi-skip with rubbish – and I spent days burning and shredding all the work-related confidential information, going back years, that was stuffed in Donald's car and his 'man-cave' shed. I've given away boxes and bagfuls of clothes, books – anything that could be useful for someone. But now, as I get closer to the completion of the practical tasks at least, I am tired beyond tired. I have no word to describe how tired I am. My bones hurt.

So I sit down in the conservatory and close my eyes. Something startles me – a noise, perhaps? – and my eyes snap open and I'm instantly awake. And I'm not in the conservatory.

I'm back in what I've come to think of as 'The Dragon Field'. I'm going to meet them this time, I feel sure. I know where I went wrong last time. I assumed I might have to confront them, do battle with them, so presented myself both defensively and aggressively. And I think I offended the dragons. Or saddened them. At any rate they didn't stay, and I felt reproached by them, that I'd pained them by my false assumptions.

But I know what I need to do this time. I don't need armour and weapons. I need to entertain them! So, much as I dislike it, I'll put the clown costume back on – I'll be the Auguste clown, I think – more colourful, more flamboyant. And here I am, in my bright orange wig and huge orange clown shoes – I'm beginning to feel hounded by the colour orange. Why all this orange?

As I ask the question, the answer comes to me. I may have mentioned that I have always had an interest in healing body and mind and have, in my time, been a reiki practitioner and teacher. Within reiki, you learn about the chakra system, an idea drawn from Eastern traditions of medicine and meditation. The chakras, or wheels, are seen as energy centres within the body, and orange is the colour of the sacral chakra that governs, among other things, creativity, sensuality and the emotional body. What other colour could I have chosen?

'*Let me entertain you…*' I sing as I see the dragons beginning to form, to assume their solid shape in their now familiar circle around me. They smile – can dragons smile? Well, these can. They smile, but I see that once again they are beginning to shake their heads, to fade from sight. Quickly I change into the White-faced Clown outfit, but even this doesn't help. The dragons have gone. I've got it wrong again.

Why can't they just tell me what they want from me? I hear a dragonish whisper in my mind – *You have to work it out for yourself.*

The other clowns have come to join me. Knowing nothing of dragons, they are pleased to see an old friend. 'Where did you sneak off to?' they say, and, 'Are you coming back to the circus?' I'm not, I explain, just visiting – but I've brought a bottle of Laphroaig with me and we can sit on the grass and talk about old times…

HIATUS: HOW AM I?

The nature of my illness means that I am often in pain, and this neuropathic pain can be severe. It mainly affects my hands and arms and legs and feet. It is often worse at night – perhaps because there are fewer distractions – and first thing in the morning. The messages travelling from my limbs to my brain and from my brain to my limbs become tangled, confused, have to find ways around the areas of demyelination along my nerve fibres. Sometimes the pain is sharp and piercing; sometimes it is like repeated electric shocks. At its worst, though, it is heavy, constant and unchanging. It feels as if my arms and legs are turning to wood or stone, and I become even clumsier than I usually am. Medication hasn't helped. I've been over-sedated, or my ankles have swollen so I am unable to get my shoes on. Cannabis – which works well for neuropathic pain – leaves me feeling uncomfortably light-headed, and seems to make my balance problems worse. In the end, I've found it easier to manage the pain than to have to manage the side effects of the medication taken to relieve the pain. I like to keep a clear head. I'm exhausted all the time, anyway – I don't want to take something that makes me even more tired. And I need to put my shoes on so I can walk my dogs!

But I do have some strategies to manage the pain and to help me with the clumsiness. I know that if I leap out of bed when I wake up, I'm quite likely to find that my legs won't support me. I could fall. So I take a few minutes just to ask myself how I am today, to take my time. I settle and centre myself as comfortably as I can and follow my breathing for a minute or two. And then I might start at my feet and work up through my body, or at my head and work down – it depends how I feel. If my mind is racing – often the case since I first read Lollipop Linda's text and became aware of Lovely Donald's hidden lives – then I start at my head. If I am more than usually tired, then I start at my feet.

Today I started with my feet. I pay attention to each part of my body in turn, checking out how my feet are, noticing any areas of pain or heaviness. I know that resisting my experience, trying to fight it, only makes things worse – rather like turning up to meet the dragons dressed in a suit of armour and brandishing a sword. If I focus all my attention on any pain I find, then that pain fills my awareness, excluding anything else – so I breathe into the areas of heaviness and discomfort, soothing and softening the sensations if I can. Then I seek out anything that might be pleasant in my immediate physical experience. This morning, for example, I noticed that my legs were less painful than usual, and this felt pleasant. My arms felt even worse than usual, but the headache I've had for a couple of days had lifted. I spent much of yesterday applying a second coat of paint to my tiny upstairs bathroom, and I noticed that the aches and pains I'd expected as the price I would have to pay for this extra activity hadn't, in fact, materialised. The relief! As I move my awareness around my body,

I realise that although I might be in pain, my physical experience isn't wholly unpleasant. There are always some positive aspects to it. And by the time I've moved my awareness around my whole body, I know how I am, where I am with my balance and energy levels, whether I need to take particular care in moving. I know how best to begin my day with a focus on ability rather than disability, while making all necessary allowances for my physical limitations in order to maximise what I can do and minimise my risk of falling.

I also observe the thoughts come into my mind and pass out again. I notice any emotions that arise and subside. I let them come and let them go – all things are passing. I remind myself that I cannot control my thoughts and emotions any more than I can control my illness, but I can control how I respond – whether to thoughts and emotions or to pain, both physical and mental. I have a choice about how to respond. Thoughts are just thoughts.

I think that Lovely Donald probably wished me dead, in the heat of his affair with the Lollipop Lady. That way everyone – my family, our friends, even, perhaps, my son – would have wished him well, wanted him to remarry. He would have been able to continue in ministry, as long as he glossed over how long he'd known the Lollipop Lady and kept quiet about the dating site – no problem, I think, for such practised and accomplished liars. These thoughts generate anger, rage, a desire to lash out, but the feelings quickly subside into a sadness deep enough for me to drown in it. These are thoughts and emotions. They feel like facts. Does that mean they are facts? They may be; they may not. I will never know – so let them go, wait for them to pass.

Take my awareness elsewhere. No point wasting time and energy on unanswerable questions and things I am powerless to change. Let the feelings be what they are until they settle of their own accord – as they will. I work towards equanimity and sometimes I almost achieve it.

So this process of scanning through my body also helps calm my mind, helps me stand back from my experience rather than being engulfed by it – and it can help me get to sleep on those nights when pain or sadness or troubling thoughts keep me awake. It's not perfect – nothing is perfect – so it doesn't work every time. But it works most of the time. It has a pretty good batting average.

It works for me. It might work for you – you'll never know unless you try it.

– 27 –

MAYBE WE AREN'T COMPLETELY FINISHED WITH MY DARK SIDE...

It's possible we aren't totally done with my Dark Side, I suppose. I've not had much time to write in the last few days, but I have had a lot of time to think. Those windmills I mentioned earlier have been clattering around like little good 'uns. I've been revolving in my mind what, if anything, I should say about some of these thoughts. Perhaps they don't exactly reflect well on me. May sound a little petty and irrelevant? I'm not sure, but I'd be interested in your opinion. Maybe it is my Dark Side at work; maybe it is a perfectly reasonable point of view. Lovely Donald suggested I am snobbish and elitist – maybe we could have a vote on whether or not he was right?

I'm sensing your impatience now. You want to know what I'm rabbiting on about. Well, it's this. There seems to me to be something irredeemably sleazy, even sordid, about married people cold-bloodedly and with premeditation setting out to find a fuck buddy on an internet dating site. They are certainly deceiving their spouses, and may be deceiving the people they meet online by misrepresenting themselves as single. They may, like Lovely Donald, be truthful about their marital status and their intentions in posting their profile. It seems that there are many people out there who are just looking for a spot of no-strings adultery.

Am I wrong to find that sleazy? It feels quite different from affairs that arise from propinquity and opportunity, where nobody has set out to betray anyone. One thing leads to another and, whoops! You are having an affair you didn't necessarily set out to have. I'm not condoning that, either, but it does feel (to me) to be less heinous than deliberately seeking out affairs – presumably with anyone who is willing – online.

Before you protest, let me be absolutely clear. I have no problem at all with internet dating sites – for single people. I think they are a very useful resource, given that our busy lives may leave little opportunity to meet potential partners any other way. I know several people who have used dating sites, with mixed results. Some have met their life partner; some have not found a serious long-term relationship but have had fun along the way; one or two have had unhappy experiences. I know my highly selective sample of users of dating sites, based on my friends and relatives, is probably unrepresentative of users as a whole, but my overall impression of dating sites for single people is generally favourable. Let me stress again here – I am talking about single people, not those who are married or in long-term relationships.

Lovely Donald was not single. Nor was Lollipop Linda. And that's bad enough. However, it felt as if Lovely Donald, without my knowledge or consent, had put me among people I would not have chosen to be associated with. Let's be clear again. I am not talking about the prostitutes here. By and large, prostitutes are doing a job – sometimes a dangerous job – often from the need to earn a living and the lack of opportunity to earn it any other way. Some may choose to be sex workers for reasons of their own. As long as they make their choices freely and are not under duress, then that's fine, isn't it?

There are many reasons why people use prostitutes, not all of them straightforwardly about sex. Lovely Donald seems to have needed what may for him have been the aphrodisiac of danger, risk, doing something illicit. Lovely Lollipop Linda did not, in fact, save him from massage parlours; as I have looked for his Will and for financial information, I have found a couple of membership cards for massage parlours dangerously close to home and work. Surprisingly recent too. It occurred to me to wonder if any of women he met in this way ever turned up at a wedding, funeral or baptism he conducted. And how he would have reacted if they did. How they would have reacted – he was very distinctive and recognisable in appearance. You wouldn't mistake him for anyone else. I've often been told that I have an inappropriate sense of humour, but I can't help smiling at the thought of Donald in his clerical garb shaking hands at the church door with a woman whose services he may have bought the night before. If it ever happened, I hope she found it amusing. I doubt Lovely Donald would have been laughing.

(On reading this through later, I'm having second thoughts. Would he, in fact, have been quite excited by such a deception being played out in front of an audience? I'm not sure.)

And I've wandered off again, so I bring my mind back and wonder what I might be avoiding? There are correspondences, after all, between me and Lovely Donald and his Lollipop Lady. I too was guilty of adultery, albeit more than thirty-eight years ago and for a few months rather than years. I didn't go looking for an affair – but adultery is always a choice and even at the time I knew I had a choice. And I chose the path of adultery, didn't enjoy it and learned that as Lovely Donald said years later, I was a rubbish liar. I'm questioning now whether I am being sophistical in making a distinction between a *normal* affair, arising from attraction and opportunity, and making a deliberate choice to put a profile up on a dating site with the intention of finding a co-adulterer. I wonder what your thoughts are? I'm aware that in making the distinctions I've made, I've based them on my feelings rather than my thinkings, so feel free to disagree with me...

Nonetheless, my feeling now is that the people with whom I would not choose to be associated are those who are willing to lie, cheat and cold-bloodedly look for adultery. People like Lovely Donald and Lollipop Linda. It is their coldness, their premeditation that leaves me shocked and buffering. And it gets worse. Lollipop Linda was a married foster parent, employed by a local authority, who not only put her photo – standing outside her house! – up on an open dating site, but then took back home the man she met there in order to have sex in her marital bed. Now maybe I'm wrong to think that this could, potentially, have been a safeguarding issue had the local child protection services been aware of it – what do you think? 'But I'm not a paedophile!' said Lovely Donald indignantly when I raised this issue. And I'm confident that this was the one thing he didn't lie about. He wasn't a paedophile. Isn't that fortunate?

But Donald had, in his time, worked in child protection and been involved professionally in painful and difficult childcare issues. He was well aware of child protection and safeguarding procedures. It seems to me that Linda showed pitifully poor judgement in signalling her availability online while still working as a foster parent, and Lovely Donald showed pitifully poor judgement in involving himself with someone prepared to behave in that way.

This might sound strange. This might be strange – but I think I might have felt a little better if Linda had been someone, in my mother's phrase, 'with a bit more about her'. Adultery always involves rejection of one kind or another and rejection, like betrayal and deceit, is hurtful. I found it added an extra dimension of hurt to be rejected in favour of someone prepared to behave as Linda did, and someone whose main attraction for Lovely Donald, apart from her availability, seemed to be that she offered him 'no intellectual challenge'.

'Surely there were other women, ones who weren't married foster parents?' I said.

'I wasn't that much of a catch,' said Lovely Donald. 'I had to take what I could get.' Once again – buffering.

Why did Lovely Donald call me snobbish and elitist? Well, it came after I said, 'It's all a bit Jeremy Kyle, isn't it?' Sorry. It was a snap judgement made in the heat of the moment. And I want to smile. Maybe I do have an inappropriate sense of humour.

You and I may disagree. You may think it acceptable for married people to cruise internet dating sites. You may even be a married person doing exactly that yourself. More clichés – I'm good at clichés. We're all different. One man's meat is another man's poison. Each to his/her own. And so on. If we differ, you can have your opinion and I will have mine. And I think it's sleazy.

Lovely Donald: 'You will think all this is tacky and immature.' It was usually Lovely Donald, though, much more than me, who criticised what he saw as other people's sexual misconduct. Once again, I can only laugh. It beats crying.

This next bit is kind of an afterthought, added after my book was finished. A persistent memory has kept niggling away at me and is demanding to be included.

I remember various conversations with my son about polyamory, when he would have been in his late twenties and polyamory was being talked about in the media. He had an interest in polyamory, albeit more theoretical than practical, and would suggest it as a possible alternative to traditional monogamy. Given the current divorce rate, he would argue, alternative models for close relationships needed to be considered. I would put forward what I saw as the pitfalls – how do people deal with jealousy? Feelings of insecurity? Child-rearing and finances? All of the complicated baggage of relationships? My son would talk about the honesty that has to be part of polyamorous relationships in order for them to work, how everyone involved has to look at how they function in relation to other people, work on their own emotional development... The differences between polyamory and cheating on a partner...

Lovely Donald, if he was present, would usually try to close down these conversations, and later took me to task for 'encouraging' our adult son to take an interest in something so unacceptable. I'd protest that I was neither encouraging or discouraging him – we were having a conversation, as grown-ups, about social trends and human relationships. Lovely Donald continued to disapprove. I shouldn't be talking about such things.

Like I said above, I can only laugh. It beats crying.

– 28 –

PAUSE: REWIND

Today would have been Lovely Donald's birthday.

This day in 2018 was the first time in thirty-five years that I had not bought him a birthday card, spent time thinking about a present for him and, in the years up to 2016, reminded Murf of the date. I asked myself how I felt, not doing any of these things, and the honest answer was that I didn't feel much of anything. Had Donald survived, I couldn't imagine that I'd have been shopping for a birthday card or present. Whilst walking the dogs round the lake that day, confirming that there were only two cygnets, not three, I felt suddenly and overwhelmingly sad. I felt, I realised, as if I was grieving for Lovely Donald as well as the missing cygnet – but, as the person I thought I knew was a construct, did not exist, for whom could I be grieving? It's complicated…

His seventieth birthday, when we were in Wales in September 2017, was a bit of a washout. We ended up having a meal in a pub near to where we were staying. It was an old, interesting pub and the food was good – it was all okay – but we weren't able to spend the day as Donald had wished. The relentless downpour made it unappealing to take the dogs to the beach or go for a walk, or do much of anything except go back to the cottage and put the heating on. I felt sad. The day felt sad. The rain poured down. Donald insisted he'd enjoyed his birthday. After tea, the weather improved and we drove to the nearest beach. The tide was in, but we went for a short walk along the cliffs with the dogs straining on their leads.

I said earlier that Donald and Linda have stolen all my memories of my marriage and, I realise, this seems to be true in a literal sense as well as metaphorically. I literally cannot remember any of Lovely Donald's birthdays over the years we spent together apart from that birthday in Wales, and his sixtieth birthday in 2007. I've spent some time today searching for memories of his birthdays and found – nothing. He must have had them; we must have done something. It's all lost now.

Friend Dick… (Sshh, now. I hear some of you hissing and booing at the mention of Friend Dick's name. I sympathise – but let me get on with the story.) Friend Dick told me repeatedly over the last months of Donald's life that in supporting Donald in his affair with Linda, Dick had 'just wanted him to have a bit of love' (me being the cold, unloving person that I am, presumably). That has made me reflect a lot on what Donald, Friend Dick and maybe even Linda meant by *love*. We use the same word, but I don't think we have the same emotion in our minds or hearts. For me, love means sharing, building something, considering the other person's wants and needs as well as your own, being in the ordinariness of everyday life together. It means being honest and accepting the difficult times as well as the good times. It means acknowledging and making allowances for each other's virtues and failings – nobody is perfect. I'm not sure what love meant for Donald, Friend Dick or even Linda – something different, I guess.

I remember Donald's sixtieth birthday very clearly. My sisters, a friend and I put a lot of effort into planning a party for him, inviting all the people he knew from all his overlapping circles of work, church, family, friendship groups. Linda, Donald's half-sister, came. I didn't invite Lollipop Linda, of course, because I was ignorant of her existence. This may have been around the time that her husband – let's call him Poor Hubby, as we have to call him something and that's how I think of him – Poor Hubby walked in on Lollipop Linda and Lovely Donald having sex on his living-room floor – or at least that's where Donald said they were. Apparently, after Donald made his hurried exit, Poor Hubby threatened to make his way over to where we lived and tell me what he'd seen. I wish he had done as he threatened – it could have made an interesting and unexpected piece of performance art at the party. And it might have saved me much grief. Linda dissuaded him, with difficulty – 'I did not want Donald to lose everything and you to be upset,' she told me. 'We'll have to be more careful now,' is what she seems to have told Donald. Donald said Hubby would never have dared confront him, anyway – he'd never been remotely worried about that. Poor Hubby! Imagine walking into your own home and finding your wife of thirty-plus years having sex on the carpet with a large, fat vicar. It must have been a shock. As well as an invasion of his home. I joke – it's what I do – but I genuinely feel for Poor Hubby, even though he did, in the end, keep secrets he should, perhaps, have shared with me.

We planned to have Lovely Donald's sixtieth birthday party at the vicarage, and a couple of people from the congregation helped with the arrangements alongside my Cucumber sister and my Huggy sister. We spent a long time planning a menu and I shopped for a mountain of food and drink. We had a frantic couple of days cooking – we wanted it all to be, not perfect – that's impossible – but lovely. We tried to include all Donald's favourite foods. Friend Dick and his wife came, but I guess Dick didn't see all the effort that had gone into the occasion (harder for me than it might sound because of my illness), or else he didn't define all this effort as love. In my terms, the effort came from a place of love – otherwise why make it? – but Donald and Dick saw things differently.

The party appeared to be a success. Donald appeared to be happy to be made a fuss of and praised by so many people. Of course, he probably would have preferred to be somewhere else, with someone else, doing something else – maybe having a burger up on Ilkley Moor, who knows? But I knew none of this. I thought I was doing, in his phrase, 'a nice thing' for him, to mark a landmark birthday. I believed his happy face, and this made the effort worthwhile. I'd have known better if I'd noticed all the times he'd come home smelling of sex and Yorkshire – but I didn't.

And this brings me to the central sadness of how I grieve

for Lovely Donald – not the person he turned out to be but the person I believe he had the potential to be if only he could have stayed honest. Over the years, I now realise, I invested far more than he did in our marriage – not that it is difficult to invest more than nothing. I tried to live up to the values expressed in his sermons about the best thing parents can do for their children. 'The best thing parents can do for their children,' he preached, many times in many sermons, 'is to love one another. This is not always as easy as it sounds. It takes effort and commitment and unselfishness on both sides...' He wasn't wrong, was he? I know I often failed – nobody is perfect – but I did try. When the time came to cash in my investment, there was less there than I'd expected or believed – but I did have the strengths I'd developed over the years and the sense that I'd done the best I could in difficult and challenging circumstances. There was something for me to draw out. I'd never criticised Donald to other people behind his back; I'd never been unfaithful; I'd tried to make it work as best I could.

For Lovely Donald, though, there was nothing. The relationship I'd thought we'd had did not exist and, once I knew this, Lovely Donald had no one to rely on, nothing to sustain him. His watertight compartments had only ever had any reality in his thinking – life can never really be that way – and he suddenly and completely saw what that meant for him. He hadn't truly invested in his relationship with Linda or any of the Lindas or, more worryingly, in his relationship with any of his children. It was, as he said himself, all smoke and mirrors. He was alone, with nothing. And I grieve for that. It was such a sad end to his life. As I think he realised, any grief that we, his closest family, feel for him is mixed with what I can only call relief and confusion. It's hard to grieve for someone so hidden and unknowable and it's hard to know how any of us could have related to him had he survived. And we are, after all, decent people who would have struggled to leave him old and ill and alone. I believe he chose to die because he could not face the future that awaited him and the destruction of the image of himself that he'd built in our minds. And now I'm crying again – just give me a couple of minutes…

Okay. Let's continue. I grieve for the person who, I truly believe, Lovely Donald could have been had he made different choices. And as more and more information came to light – I read some of the emails, Friend Dick let one or two details slip, by accident? Deliberately? – other bits of information came my way. It became obvious that every conversation I'd had with Lovely Donald in the last four months of his life was full of lies on his part – his default mode was to lie. And I grieve for that too. He could, as I told him, have been honest. I'd have found forgiveness for the things he'd done far more easily than I could find forgiveness for the lies.

'I should have talked to you years ago, and not to Dick,' said Donald on New Year's Eve, a time of new beginnings. But he hadn't. And he still didn't. I grieve that the very last conversation I ever had with Donald was one in which he just lied and lied – what was the point at that stage?

I've been thinking today about Stephen Karpman's Drama Triangle of persecutor-rescuer-victim. I must take some responsibility for the way we became stuck, tempting as it is to just blame Donald. He was stuck, most of the time, in victim mode in his thinking and, just like his first wife, I moved from rescuer to persecutor in his world view. And all unknown to me, I became stuck as the persecutor as far as Donald was concerned. I knew I'd begun in rescuer mode, but I guess, if I'd been asked, I might have said that maybe we'd escaped the triangle. But we hadn't – and so we all became victims in the end, one way or another. I can't, just now, bear to think about where Murf might have fitted into this, but I will, later. Probably alone.

For now, though, I've been reflecting on the only two of Lovely Donald's birthdays for which I can find any memories and reflecting, too, on how sad it is that all the other memories have fled – or maybe they just went *pop*, as my unreal life went *pop*. There is only sadness.

But I want to pass on a warning too. If, as you are reading this, you are finding correspondences between your own marriage or relationship and mine, look more closely at your own life. If you realise that you are the only person who is really putting any effort into the relationship, interrogate that realisation. If you hear the persistent tinkling of little warning bells, however distant they seem and however busy you might be, listen to them. Work out what they are trying to tell you. What do you need to do? I know I've said this before, but perhaps it merits repetition?

And today will soon be over. Lovely Donald's birthday will have passed. I have paid him a necessary tribute of grief, despite everything, and that will continue. As he lay in hospital on the morning of his death, his friend and fellow clergyman gave him the last rites, asked for his sins to find forgiveness as he reached the end of his life. I'm told that our hearing is the last of our senses to fade, so I hope Lovely Donald could hear the familiar words and that they brought him some comfort.

– 29 –

DOUBLE, DOUBLE...

I am the eldest of four children, or six, depending on how you count it. My mother lost two babies in the first days of their lives. We can use their real names – they should be heard. Stephen and Abigail.

My youngest sister died in 2004, and so now we are three. Lovely Donald used to compare us to the *Graeae*, or three Grey Sisters, of Greek mythology. The *Graeae* were sisters to the Gorgons, whose secret they were forced to betray. They were born as old women, and shared but a single eye and a single tooth between them. They were deceived by a man – doesn't that feel kind of inevitable? Perseus, on his way to face Medusa the Gorgon, stole their one eye, leaving them all sightless. He held it to ransom until they told him how Medusa could be killed. Understandably enough, Perseus did not want to fall victim to Medusa's superpower, which was the ability to turn to stone anyone who looked at her. You remember Medusa, don't you? She's the one with the writhing snakes in place of hair (an image that gave me nightmares as a child, though Murf loved it).

Lovely Donald had to admit that my Huggy Sister, my Cucumber Sister and myself had a full complement of eyes and teeth. The question he used to ask when we were together was about who was in possession of the family brain cell today? The wine would flow and even when we were much younger, we would cackle like crones as we riffed off each other, laughing at life and ourselves. Sometimes Lovely Donald would join in, and sometimes not. He seemed very much a part of what went on, usually in the kitchen of whoever's house we happened to be in at the time. His frequently repeated question, 'Who has the family brain cell today?', became a standing joke over many, many years. It seemed like affectionate banter. I've no idea, now, what was in his mind, or whether his seeming affection for all of us had any foundation in reality. When he joked about the family brain cell, was there an added layer in his amusement from his knowledge that he was deceiving us all? That we didn't see through him? Or was he, in that moment, the person he appeared to be, participating in family life, enjoying our company? I go back to buffering.

And I buffer myself away to a blasted heath, dark, mysterious and cold. Shrubs and trees take on strange shapes in the darkness – are they really shrubs, or something more sinister? Are they moving? Bats fly overhead. Owls hoot in the darkness as another small mammal meets its death.

My sisters and I move in rhythm round our cauldron, as the fire crackles and burns underneath it, illuminating a small space around us, adding to the sense of movement in the shadows… Our trailing black garments fly out as we move; our hair streams behind us. Our tall, pointed hats are quite tricky to keep in place, but we've managed it with a few judiciously placed hairpins.

We are not afraid. We are at home, here in the darkness. We are crones, the final phase of the Triple Goddess – the post-menopausal women who have nothing to prove and nothing to fear. We see past and future, both contained in the present, without distinction. Past, present and future are all one, we realise. As we move round the cauldron, we chant our endless song:

Double, double, toil and trouble,
Fire burn and cauldron bubble…

And arrogant as it may seem to rewrite Shakespeare, we really don't want any fillets of fenny snake or tongue of dog in our cauldron. Tongue of dog? I hope my terriers are not reading this over my shoulder as they sit beside me on the bench. Ours is a vegan cauldron – just as effective for casting a spell here on the blasted heath at the fell of midnight. And we cast our spells not to gain power or the possession of secrets, never for harm, but for the protection of those we love. Who might all be better off with a healthy, planet-saving vegan diet.

Double, double, toil and trouble,
Fire burn and cauldron bubble…
Some puy lentils let us take,

With some onions, boil and bake,
Mushrooms, grown on mossy log,
Picked when midnight's wreathed in fog,
Let's chuck in those green cucumbers,
Carrots, too, in larger numbers,
Peppers, spinach, add more veggies –
Where's those sweet potato wedges?
Curry spices, strong and hot,
In they go – and we forgot!
More green chillis – four and twenty,
Some scotch bonnets – five, that's plenty.
Double, double toil and trouble,
Fire burn! And cauldron bubble.
Sisters, join our hands and voices,
Hope for wise and clever choices,
Round the cauldron dance we three.
Seal the spell. So mote it be!
Double, double, toil and trouble,
Fire burn and cauldron bubble…

And actually it is cold out here on the heath. I'm not sure cucumbers are a good addition to our cauldron. Maybe we'd be better off in my kitchen with a bottle of wine? Or there's gin? I might even share the Laphroaig…

We can have a good cackle together and forget our troubles for a time. We can rejoice in the solidarity of sisters together, here, now, in this moment.

– 30 –

LOLLIPOP LINDA AND FRIEND DICK

Did they ever meet, I wonder, Lollipop Linda and Friend Dick? Both say not, but I'll never really know, will I? And I realise it doesn't matter anyway.

In the last few days, a couple of people have asked me how I feel about Lollipop Linda now. That's made me think. How DO I feel about Lollipop Linda now?

It's complicated. I've already explained that I struggle to find respect for people who behave as she did, who trivialise and cheapen human relationships. I'm not impressed by her forays into online dating for married people, affairs with married men, her invasion of my marriage, my home, my life and, not content with all that – why does this bother me so much? – walking my dogs. They are well-brought-up so unfailingly friendly to everyone they meet, but I'd have forgiven them if they'd bitten her or peed on her shoes. I have to remember, though, that she seems to have had no compunction about taking Lovely

Donald into her house and into the bed she shared with her husband, albeit not until their second meeting, he assured me. She went on to deceive her husband for some years, so why on earth would she have hesitated to walk my dogs?

So what I feel – in flashes, red, jagged moments – is rage. But it doesn't stick. I can't sustain it, and I'm not sure why.

Somehow, when I think of Lollipop Linda, I see her, in my mind's eye, reduced in size, little, not quite a whole person. I cannot escape a lurking feeling that she knew no better, and somehow that arouses in me a kind of pity. She didn't think of Lovely Donald's family or her own, she said. She was unhappy in her marriage and wanted to feel needed. Lovely Donald's desire for transgressive sex gave her, for a time, the feeling of being needed. And so I find myself, obscurely and inexplicably, feeling sorry for her. (Sorry, Cucumber Sister. I know that if you are reading this, you probably want to smack me – hard – at this moment. But that's how I feel.)

I don't see Linda as a predatory homewrecker, but as someone who, like the rest of us, wanted to avoid suffering and find pleasure. And if we are consumed by our thoughts and emotions, unable to stand back for a moment and think about consequences, then we have nothing to guide our actions. And that feels sad.

Something, too, in the way Lovely Donald spoke of Linda aroused some strange kind of almost protective instinct in me. There seemed something demeaning to both of them in his language and tone, and the attitudes that seemed to underlie his words. She was 'no intellectual challenge', he said and, he admitted, he enjoyed feeling superior to both her and her husband. As time passed, though, said Lovely Donald, Linda made no demands on him – never asked him to take out the rubbish, help in the house, clear the weeds from the garden, offer emotional support when she needed it rather than when he wanted to offer it – and all that made her lovable. I was unlovable because I did make demands, even though those demands seemed reasonable to me at the time. (*Can we just clean your office before the Diocesan Property Manager comes for his quinquennial inspection of the vicarage?*)

Eventually I accused Lovely Donald of exploiting someone who sounded, from his description of her background and personality, to be quite needy and vulnerable.

No such thing, Lovely Donald insisted. Certainly he was using her – but she was using him too. 'We were using each other,' he said. It was a game. They both knew the rules of this game. Each would say *nice things* to the other, so that the other would say *nice things* back, but with no depth or meaning behind the words. In this game you say 'I love you' so the other person will say the same to you. It feels good to hear the words, but they don't have to have any great meaning or significance in your wider life. 'It was not the kind of relationship to lead to anything,' said Lovely Donald. 'It wasn't going anywhere.' 'It didn't take up much time or attention,' he said. In that case, I asked, why not just stop? Silence.

Of course, Lovely Donald may simply have been lying yet again, telling me what he thought I wanted to hear, but I suppose I felt something cold, exploitative, unwholesome, more in his demeanour than in the actual words he used. If it was, as he said, all a game, I can't help feeling that Donald might have been playing with a stacked deck.

I really can't explain this because I don't understand it at all, but as I listened to Lovely Donald talk about Linda, I saw Komodo dragons stalking their prey for days, waiting for the poison in their first bite to take effect, to weaken the buffalo to the point where it cannot fight back. Then the Komodo dragon – not really a dragon but something much nastier – closes in for the kill… and feasts. But even as I talk about the nastiness of the Komodo dragon, it comes to me that from his perspective he is simply doing what he needs to do in order to survive. My sympathies are with the buffalo, but does that mean that the poor old Komodo dragon should starve?

Who was the Komodo dragon? Lovely Donald? Lollipop Linda? Both of them? Neither of them? Friend Dick, even? Me, as I write this?

I don't know. I don't suppose I'll ever know. Komodo dragons stalk through my nightmares.

So what do I feel now about Lovely Linda? Weariness, I suppose, a slight feeling of pity, some distaste. What comes to me is that she doesn't feel big enough to deserve rage – does that sound patronising? Lovely Donald trawled for women willing to join him in his game; he found Linda. As I've said before, if it hadn't been her, it would have been someone else. He carried right on trawling, it seems, until life, age and illness damaged his trawl nets to the point of uselessness.

And what has just come to me now, in this moment, is the

memory of reading Lovely Donald's emails. I read somewhere between a quarter and a third of them, not all of them. I've just realised that this wasn't only from my sense at the time that I shouldn't be reading them at all, that they were never intended for my eyes, but also because reading them induced in me a feeling close to a sort of nauseous exhaustion. Reading them felt like being trapped in an endless *Carry On* film – all bums and tits and *double entendres*. There's only so much of this that I can take. Lovely Donald always enjoyed the *Carry On* films. I tended to find that they soon became repetitive and unfunny. I found their treatment of women difficult – maybe I just take life too seriously?

Jagged lightning flashes of rage smash across my mind when I think of the possible impact on my son of the emotional hollowness and deadness at the sclerotic heart of our family. Then come hailstones as big as golfballs that pound me into the ground. My son, my son.

But I can't really blame Lollipop Linda for any of this. As she said herself, she never gave a thought to my son or to me. She didn't know us, after all, never met us. We were nothing to her. Why waste concern on unknown others?

Lovely Donald, on the other hand, knew the theory. He preached the sermon, often at weddings, about the effort, commitment and unselfishness required in marriage and parenthood. Preaching is one thing – putting those values into practice is quite another. But then don't we all fail to practise what we preach at times? What matters, said Lovely Donald, is your intention...

I am, long-windedly, reaching a conclusion to this chapter, I promise.

I suppose that Linda now feels like a bit of an irrelevance. I don't have too much energy to waste on her. I have no respect for her behaviour, but, like all of us, she is a human being and was probably doing what she felt she needed to do at the time. (Though as my stepson has pointed out, I could make a distinction between needs and wants.) It would be comforting – but wrong – to blame her, at least in part, for the tragedy of my son's life and death and the disappearance of my life as I knew it. Thoughtless, careless people cause damage, not least to themselves, but she is what she is, and I am what I am. I stayed in an unfulfilling marriage – my choice. I allowed myself to be lulled by the face Lovely Donald prepared to enable him to meet the world.

Is it possible, in fact, that Lovely Donald was wrong? That sometimes, in truth, the best thing parents can do for their children is to let go of effort and commitment – and just leave? Might my son still be alive if I'd had the sense to do that? And here's another unanswerable, so largely pointless, question.

I'm falling yet again into what psychologists call 'the hindsight bias', the 'I knew it all the time' phenomenon. This is a form of cognitive distortion in which an outcome or event, once it has happened, becomes, in our minds, much more obvious and predictable than it actually was at the time. 'If only I'd done something different.' 'If only I'd left Lovely Donald.'

But I didn't. And, as my mother always said, the saddest words in the English language are 'if only'. The choices I made seemed, based on the information available to me at the time, to be the choices that were best for all of us. In the same situation, given the same information, and believing as I did that Lovely Donald's words represented his feelings and values, I would probably make the same choices all over again. And anyway, we can never know how life would have turned out if I'd made different choices. It's easy to assume it would have been better – but who knows?

And I was going to write about Friend Dick in this chapter, but I suddenly feel very tired. I haven't had my breakfast and I'm hungry. I need to leave all this for now, eat some porridge and walk the dogs. I can come back to Friend Dick later. He can have a chapter all to himself. It will be a short one.

– 31 –

FRIEND DICK

Oh dear. I said this chapter would be a short one. I realise I was mistaken. Here's your health warning: it will be a long read. Maybe pause now, get yourself some chocolate (I recommend Montezuma dark chocolate with sea salt and lime.) Maybe a glass of wine. Or a cup of camomile tea. Prepare for a long haul.

Since I began writing what we are now calling my book, my audience has widened from me and my therapist to include those members of my family who want to read it, a couple of friends and one or two other people on a need-to-know basis. Their interest has encouraged me to continue when I might have wearied of the effort. The response from one of my niblings – can you guess the gender of this person? – was interesting. 'The person I hate most in all this?? DICK.' And, yes, you're right – she's a she.

I understand her response because I feel the same. Of course, this feeling will have influenced my thoughts and my choice of words, however much I have tried to be fair in my presentation of the *dramatis personae* in this – what? Tragedy? Comedy? Farce? Soap opera? Autobiography? And the words I choose will naturally influence my niece's response – yours too. Take nothing on trust. Examine what I say. If there are moments when you suspect that I am manipulating your emotions, your thoughts – interrogate that. Don't feel you have to accept what I say or agree with me. It's said that history is told by the victors, but that's not always true, is it? Sometimes history is told by the survivors, the only people left to tell what happened.

As for Friend Dick, there was a moment – only a moment – shortly after I saw the Lollipop text, when the thought scuttled through my mind that Friend Dick is Satan. I could hear his red tail swishing, and I had a feeling that concealed in his abundant grey hair there could be sharp, devilish horns. I saw his claws, felt their force on my skin.

It was only a moment and, in my defence, it came at a time when no one except me knew that my life had disappeared into non-existence along with gorgons and unicorns. Obviously, Lovely Donald and Friend Dick are the exceptions to that – they knew far more than I did about my unreal life. For a couple of months, they were the only people I could talk to – can you imagine that? It was not sustainable, at least not for me.

You are reading my story as I tell it. Don't forget that Lovely Donald and Friend Dick had their stories too. They would be telling you another story, in which I had brought all that happened down on my own head by being someone whom Lovely Donald simply could not love. Given that central fact, what else could he have done other than what he did? So I would be the villain in their story. (I can think of one or two other things that Lovely Donald might have done, but perhaps we'll come to that later.)

'It's the way I tell 'em.' I've remembered the name of the comedian, famous when I was young, whose catchphrase that was. Frank Carson. Imagine a Belfast accent. *It's the way I tell 'em.* So this is my version of the story and there are no villains.

Much as the image of Friend Dick with horns and a tail appeals to me, he is not Satan. He is, though, a mystery to me in many ways – a man who worked with vulnerable people, a trained counsellor, a therapist. But sometimes his words and the attitudes expressed left me breathless and speechless. Trust me, I'm not often speechless. But sometimes, when talking to Dick, I struggled to know what to say.

Lovely Donald used to refer to Friend Dick, over the years, as 'Dementia Dick' – only behind his back, of course. He used to tell me, in more detail than I wanted to hear, that he had to stay friends with Dick because otherwise Dick would be friendless. According to Donald, Dick tended to alienate people because of his right-wing views, his extreme tactlessness and his irritability and poor impulse control. Was any of this true? You tell me.

But, Donald would continue, Dick is basically a decent and well-meaning person. He deserves to have a friend, so Donald wanted to fill that gap for him. Is it just me or does that sound a tad patronising? Anyway, that's what he used to say.

The two of them played badminton together, or golf. They

met once a week and would usually go out for a meal once the sport was over. I had very little contact with Dick over most of the years of their friendship. Occasionally he and Donald would stay in. I'd make them coffee, and maybe a sandwich. They'd invite me to play Scrabble with them. I'd usually win. Dick was always friendly, looked me in the eye and talked as though he believed that Donald regarded me with affection and listened to what I had to say. If nothing else, he's a good actor.

Donald told Dick very early on that I had seen the Lollipop text. They settled on a story to tell me – very little of which was true, as I learned over the months. As new information came my way, Donald would change or modify his story and Dick would back him up.

Dick wanted to help me, he said – he could appreciate that all of this must be very painful for me, but, after all, no harm was done. Lovely Donald had not left me, had he?

It was all 'water under the bridge', said Dick. Lovely Donald had stayed with me – he and Linda had sat down together after Poor Hubby had departed the stage in 2012, and they had decided not to move in together but to continue as they were. I needed, said Dick, to understand and appreciate that they had showed some concern for me in making this decision. But, I responded, all these people knew far more about my life than I did. They made decisions that affected me without my knowledge or consent. I might have liked some say in my own life?

Now I was being silly, Dick pointed out. After all, if Lovely Donald couldn't get along with me, didn't like me, he was entitled to look elsewhere for someone more compatible, more able to meet his needs. There's no harm in that, after all, because he didn't leave me. Donald couldn't be honest because I wouldn't have liked it and I might have left. He might have had to leave ministry. People might not have understood and might have disapproved of him. And, after all, you have to tell lies and keep secrets if you are going to have affairs... And Donald had to use a dating site, didn't he? How else could he have found such a 'nice friendship' as the one he had with Linda? I knew nothing about it, he 'thought a lot of Linda', so no harm done.

Poor Donald, continued Dick, thought a lot of Linda and, anyway, he couldn't leave me because my son disliked me so much. He obviously had to stay, didn't he?

Dick seemed to think it was all so reasonable – as did Lovely Donald. It was all over now, anyway, so what on earth was I making a fuss about? What did I expect?

Poor Lovely Donald, Dick told me. He had been so unlucky. His first wife was a vicious shrew who made his life a misery however hard he tried, and then he marries again and I was no better! Poor man! And he was such a saint. He helped so many people, after all. He even helped our son financially – he deserves only admiration for all his saintly qualities.

I helped our son financially, too, but somehow this didn't seem to confer sainthood on me. Make what sense you can of that.

Picture me in shock – buffering.

But then Friend Dick ventured into dangerous territory, debatable ground. Poor Lovely Donald was such a lovely man that it was inevitable, really, that some of his relationships with his female counselling clients over the years would become something more, would turn into 'loving friendships'. And there's nothing wrong with a bit of closeness, a few lunches, after all…

Whoa! I don't remember what I said – something about professional boundaries and ethics in counselling. I know. I'm boring. But that was what came into my mind at the time.

Friend Dick babbled a bit, backtracked. Maybe it was only the very occasional lunch – no harm done. And, he added, I was being ridiculous in even allowing the thought of leaving Lovely, Lovely Donald now. I was making a fuss about nothing. He hadn't left me, had he? And sex is powerful. Poor old Lovely Donald had to find ways to meet his sexual needs, after all.

I reminded Dick that it had been Donald's choice, not mine, to put a full stop to any kind of physical life between us. Dick signalled disbelief – whatever had happened, it must have been my fault because Lovely, Lovely Donald was such a good, caring man. (Donald's subsequent explanation for bringing our sex life to a halt was that, because of his encounters with other women, he felt unclean, unworthy to approach me. No, I didn't believe him, either.)

All that is irrelevant, anyway, said Dick. Donald was ill now, after all. (So am I – but there I go again, bringing in yet more irrelevancies.) Linda wasn't offering to help Donald, said Dick – she couldn't, after all. She was with someone else now – a man who owns six cars. (Why did the number of cars matter? No idea. It seemed to matter to Dick.) I was Donald's wife, after all, so it was my responsibility to stay with him now that he needed help.

Yet again Dick stressed my good fortune – Lovely Donald

had chosen to stay with me and had said repeatedly to Dick that the last three faithful years had been the happiest of his life.

How? I asked. We'd spent the last three years watching our son being driven to oblivion, powerless to help him. Donald had made my life a misery in many ways, not least his refusal to seek medical advice in the face of ever-worsening symptoms. I reminded Dick of the hard time he himself had given me repeatedly – asking why didn't I make Lovely Donald sort out his medical issues as if he really believed that Donald cared anything for my views. Maybe, I suggested, he should have had those conversations with Linda? Or not had them at all?

Dealing with my son's death and its aftermath wasn't enough, he seemed to suggest. I had to take responsibility not just for my own health, but for Lovely Donald's too. It was obviously my fault that Donald had been unable or unwilling to address the problems that had arisen. I reminded Dick that Donald had refused to listen to anyone – me, Dick, his sons. Well, said Dick, if I'd been a proper wife, he'd have listened.

The last three years, I repeated, have not been happy. Dick shrugged. I didn't understand. He was right about that.

I am reporting this as a single conversation, but it was actually a series of conversations spread over the last four months of Donald's life up to his death and funeral. Sorry, I forgot the 'Lovely'. Dick never forgot to stress the loveliness of Donald, his goodness, his all-round excellence.

I doubted my sanity at moments. My sisters, once they knew about Lovely Donald's secret life, asked the same question in exactly the same words:

'Who is this Dick? Why, in God's name, are you talking to this man?'

Because, for more than six weeks, I had no one else to talk to. I told nobody what I'd learned, not even my son. I still write to him several times a week, just keeping him up to date with world affairs, family news and day-to-day stuff. I'd told him about his father's illness, but I hadn't mentioned Linda, or Stephanie or the massage parlours or any of it.

I could have told my son. After all, I could rely on him to respect my confidences and not repeat anything I said to him. I didn't want to upset him, or worry him, and so I didn't tell him. Don't fret – I know he's beyond all that now. Feelings aren't always rational, though, are they? So I kept it all to myself.

I did worry, though, about how much he'd known, how that knowledge had affected him, whether he'd ever confronted his father, why he hadn't told me clearly of his suspicions. I doubt that he knew everything, or had specific facts, but that he had suspicions I am horribly certain. He did, I realise now – hindsight again! – warn me that all was not well, but so obliquely that I only understand him now, years later.

As I listened to Friend Dick, thought of my son, doubted my sanity, made my twice-daily visits to the hospital, walked my dogs and felt increasingly exhausted, there came a moment when I snapped.

'Sometimes,' said Friend Dick, in his kindly, avuncular voice, 'people don't know what is in their own best interests. I understand how you feel. I know you *think* you want to know what happened, but you have to be guided by people who know better than you do what is good for you. You need to forget about Lovely Donald's women now. It won't do you any good to know what happened and it's all over now, anyway. You just need to concentrate on how lucky you are that Lovely Donald chose to stay with you, and focus on what he needs. Forget all this nonsense about leaving. The past is the past – none of your business. Don't be silly. Just listen to people who understand better than you what you need to do now."

Enough was enough. 'Fuck off, Dick,' I said. Or is that just what I wish I'd said? Maybe I was a bit more polite.

Don't forget, too, that while I'm trying to use Dick's own words as far as possible, my memory, like yours, is fallible. I was upset. I felt patronised and talked-down to. I was angry. I don't know now whether I am always reporting Dick's words exactly as he spoke them. I am most certainly reporting how I experienced his words, what they meant to me. And at every point when my anger began to settle into something calmer, I felt as if Dick was there with a pack of firelighters, to feed the flames.

Was it just a paranoid fantasy, born of exhaustion and distress, when, just for an instant, I saw Friend Dick as Satan? Short of hunting him down and forcing him to strip so I can check for a tail, I can't be completely sure.

However, you need to remember that this is only my perception of what happened, how it felt to me. I could have been mistaken. I was distressed. I was certainly confused. Maybe I'm still confused?

Sometimes, just sometimes, I had an uncomfortable, toothache-y feeling that Dick was deliberately and with malice dropping in comments designed to make things worse. I had a feeling – just a feeling – some of the time that Dick, while expressing concern for me, was in fact enjoying my distress, suggesting to me that somehow it was all my fault, that I'd driven Lovely Donald to infidelity and deceit. That I was being ridiculous in seeing any kind of issue here at all. Think about that for a moment. Really? Dick was certainly pressurising me to keep Donald's secrets, tell nobody, not ever.

I said to him once – sarcastically – that the only way I would be able to cope with keeping Donald's secrets forever would be to move away, far from family and friends, to cut off my links with my family, my friends and my son's friends as much as I could. People were beginning to question me, to suspect that all was not well with me beyond the obvious issues they already knew about. As Lovely Donald said himself, I am a rubbish liar.

Dick didn't understand my problem with lying, but, given that I did have a problem, he thought it was an excellent idea for me to move away, cut ties with anyone and everyone who knew Lovely Donald, make a fresh start in a new place, away from anything that might tempt me to talk to people. He had, he said, my best interests at heart.

I'm not sure that's true. What do you think? Are you hearing the swish of a red satanic tail? Finding a slight whiff of sulphur in the air? Or feeling you need to call my GP and arrange a mental health assessment?

My view – I believe that Dick's relationship with Donald was a mutually destructive relationship. Each of them brought out and encouraged the worst in the other. Dick encouraged

Donald's sense of entitlement – can you really be entitled to lie and cheat? Donald begged me not to leave – but listened to Dick, who told him not to tell me what had really happened over the years.

Both men seemed totally unable to comprehend what seems to me to be completely simple and basic. Much as I might have been upset and angered by an honest account of Donald's affairs over the thirty-four years of our marriage, I was even more upset and angered by being fed lies, more lies and self-justifications. I'd have liked some guilt, some contrition, some acceptance of responsibility for damage caused – but I'd have settled for a bit of honesty.

But – and this is the most enormous 'but' that you can imagine – Friend Dick is not responsible for Donald's choices and actions. Donald's infidelities began long before he met Friend Dick, after all. Ironically, they first met some twenty years ago when both were working as counsellors/therapists in a local voluntary agency. Perhaps they were drawn together because each met a need in the other. Like Velcro, they both had the right hooks to form a bond.

I've tried to believe – I'd love to believe – that Lovely Donald was a tragic hero, a man who was basically good brought down by a single fatal flaw. That would, I suppose, make Friend Dick Iago to Lovely Donald's Othello.

That would be a comforting belief to have, would absolve Donald from at least some of the responsibility for his actions. But I don't believe it.

Donald made his own choices. His course was set long

before the SS *Friend Dick* sailed into view, flags flying, band playing, guns ready to be fired into the enemy ships – uppity women, people who don't know their place, the politically correct brigade...

Something Donald said to me maybe hints at the flavour of the relationship between the two men. It was one of the strange and chilling conversations I had with Donald, which still leave me feeling – what? Bemused. Almost afraid. Buffering.

Sometimes Donald would say something as if it was the most obvious and natural thing in the world. He would observe my response, often a silent response, because I was feeling shocked beyond words. Then he would seem to realise – I could see it in his face, hear it in his voice – that what he had just said might be perceived as shocking by more people than me. And Donald would then reflect that shock back to me, almost as if he had suddenly shocked himself. It was bizarre, surreal, unsettling. And I may not be explaining this very well. I'm doing my best. It was just my perception, my experience. I felt in these moments as if I was meeting something that could, under other circumstances, have frightened me – a coldness, a deadness that made the skin on my back crawl and the hairs on my arms stand up to attention. Even now, as I write this, I shiver, though the room is warm and my Border terrier is lying across my feet.

Anyway, I was going to tell you what Lovely Donald said, wasn't I? And you need a bit of context in order to understand why it affected me as it did.

For years, Donald has come home from his expeditions

with Dick and talked about Dick's marital disharmonies. I didn't pay much attention. It was none of my business. But it seemed to exercise Lovely Donald. The gist of it seemed to be that both Dick and his wife – let's call her Meg – have secrets. I would gently suggest to Donald that perhaps it would be more useful for Friend Dick to talk to Meg about his various issues, rather than just complaining about her behind her back. I hoped Donald didn't talk about me in this way. Donald was shocked at the very idea that he would do that – how could I think such a thing of him?

Donald would say that Dick couldn't raise the various issues directly with Meg because – wait for it! You know what I'm going to say next, don't you? Dick couldn't talk to Meg because she wouldn't understand. As I write this now, I'm wondering whether sometimes the lies we tell ourselves are the worst lies of all, the ones from which all other lies flow.

Like Meg, I didn't understand. Surely, I'd say, all these secrets and unspoken resentments take energy away from a marriage? Drive a wedge between husband and wife? 'Yes,' Lovely Donald would say, 'but that's Dick for you.'

Lovely Donald's relationship with Friend Dick was intensely competitive. You need to know this. It mattered to them both who won at badminton and golf. It annoyed the hell out of them that I could often beat both of them at Scrabble. Should I have had due regard for the male ego and let them win? Show of hands, please. Let them win? Not let them win?

Having due regard to their competitiveness, Lovely Donald explained, I needed to understand that in order to be one up on

Dick, he had to find a woman to have sex with. Dick's wife didn't understand him, just as I didn't understand Donald, but Dick hadn't had the nerve to seek consolation elsewhere. Dick might beat Donald at golf and badminton most of the time, but Donald had beaten Dick when it came to finding a woman to have sex with. I needed, said Lovely Donald, to understand how driven he had been by his need to beat Friend Dick at something.

'Are you serious?,' I asked. He was, but I could see a thought enter his mind, a doubt begin to show itself in his eyes. His hitherto unexamined certainties were, perhaps, beginning to seem not quite so certain.

I told you I have an inappropriate sense of humour. I laughed. Here were two adult men, in their fifties into their sixties and seventies, competing to see who could practise the greater deceit on their wives – and anticipating that I would see this as perfectly reasonable. What else could I do but laugh? What would you have done?

So Friend Dick was not Iago, and nor was he a pantomime villain. Despite my small vision of him in a fetching red outfit with cloven hoofs, horns and a tail, nor was he the Devil. He was, and is, a man in his seventies, an admirer of President Trump, an apologist for Harvey Weinstein et al, and a product of his times, his upbringing, his personality and past experiences. His misogyny may be, as it often is, a mask for insecurity, feelings of inferiority, fear, even – who knows? That's one possibility.

It's possible, too, that my niece has a point when she says that she thinks that '...they gravitated to each other to justify and validate a pair of misogynistic and narcissistic bastards'.

But, in the immortal words of Mandy Rice-Davies, I would say that, wouldn't I? Whatever the truth of it, thanks for the support, Nibling. ☺

I know I promised that this would be a short chapter. Sorry. We all make mistakes. These words don't always come as I expect them to come. They have a way of forcing themselves on to the page in their own way, heedless of my plans for them.

And there are almost 69,000 of the little beggars now, forming sentences and paragraphs and chapters, working hard to try to make sense of the unravelling of my life. Sometimes when you try to untangle a ball of wool, you just have to accept defeat, pick up the scissors and cut the tangle out. Then you join the ends of the wool and carry on.

I'm coming close to that point, I think, in this narrative. Questions do not always have answers, particularly when you are asking them of the dead. Life does not always make sense. Maybe there comes a point when it can be seen as self-indulgent or self-destructive, or both, to go on trying to untangle all the knots and tangles of the past. Sometimes you just have to cut out those tangles, join the ends, and carry on. Otherwise you risk losing the present.

My son was a man not like Lovely Donald or Friend Dick. Though his honesty and desire for integrity in relationships probably contributed to his death, I have to be thankful for that. My stepsons are men not like Lovely Donald or Friend Dick. I am thankful for that too.

Maybe it's time for us to return to the dragon field and visit the dragons again. It's obvious now what I should have been doing, how best to meet them. Why did it take me this long to work it out?

INTERLUDE

Last Friday felt like the first day of autumn – there was a chill in the air and the leaves were falling. Almost overnight, the trees had turned from green to red and yellow and orange, all the rich and melancholy autumn colours. I love autumn. It's my favourite season of the year. It's a time for reflection, taking stock, getting ready for the coming winter months of darkness. But on Friday the sun was shining and the sky was a clean, crisp blue – a good day for a walk.

So we went for a walk, the dogs and I. My little dog walked through the heaps of fallen leaves and seemed to enjoy the noise they made as she swished through them, scattering them quite deliberately. If a dog can smile, she was smiling. My older, bigger dog looked on indulgently, waiting to get on with the walk, but willing to let her play for a while.

A very clear memory came into my mind's eye, triggered by the cool sunshine and the sound of the leaves. My son, aged three, in his little blue coat, matching peaked hat and blue Thomas the Tank Engine wellies. He's walking along kicking up the leaves, much like my little dog, and he's laughing. 'Look! Colours!'

This is the same walk, the same kind of day, the same kind of leaves probably fallen from the self-same trees. These trees have been here for many years – longer than my son's lifetime, which wasn't very long at all.

For a moment, my son is alive again. I am back in that moment. I can see him in his little blue coat, I can hear his laughter.

My Border terrier barks to remind me to move or to ask for a doggy treat as a reward for his patience. We walk on along the path.

– 32 –

WHERE'S THE RICE PUDDING?

Words are slippery. However hard you try to pin them down into precise meaning, they slither and shapeshift. Ambiguity abounds. Misunderstanding muscles in everywhere. Words are just words – love, loyalty, family, integrity, husband, wife, commitment. We think we know what the words mean, but how can we know what they signify in the mind of another person? Lovely Donald and I used to talk about the importance of empathy and genuineness, being real in relationships. I know what I meant when I used those words. I will never know what Lovely Donald meant.

'Entertain' is another word with multiple meanings. I might say, 'I've entertained the thought that everything that's happened might in some way be my fault.' Or I might say, 'I realised the dragons wanted me to entertain them, so I put on my clown costume.' It occurs to me that I might have misunderstood what the dragons meant by 'entertain'. They don't want me in a clown suit, falling over and being assaulted with custard pies – they want a party!

A few months after my son's funeral – and it still feels incongruous to use the words 'my son' and 'funeral' in the same sentence – we held a 'Going Away Party and Final Aerial Passage' for him. It was a focus for Lovely Donald and I and for my son's family and friends in the bleakness of the landscape of his death. It was something we could do to express our solidarity in grief and celebrate my son's life in a way he would enjoy. It was a gesture of defiance too – the manner of his death did not define his life. So his friends with the big house and spare land offered a venue. His cheffy friends prepared a banquet – inevitably with lots of chillies involved. His friend with the knowledge of real ale sourced suitable barrels from the wonderfully named Anarchy Ales. Yet more friends with expertise in pyrotechnics obtained impressive fireworks, and put a portion of my son's ashes, and those of his much-loved dog, into mortar shells, to be fired, blazing, into the night sky. And once again I need to stop and breathe and find some tissues. Back in a minute.

Life contains a lot of interruptions. I meant to be back in a minute – but this happened and that happened and I'm back now, an hour and a half later.

My son's Going Away Party. I am writing this five days before the anniversary of the Going Away Party, and the imminence of the anniversary inevitably turns my thoughts back to the event. It evolved from a discussion a week after my son's death. Had he ever expressed any opinions about the kind of funeral he'd want? And he hadn't, beyond a conversation with one of his friends where they'd talked about a sky burial. That's a practice found in some other cultures where the corpse is left exposed on a high wooden platform to allow the wind, the weather and the birds to do their work. I can see the appeal, but it's a little difficult to arrange a sky burial in England. Well, said my son's friend's dad – the expert in pyrotechnics – why not send him up in a firework? That's a kind of sky burial, after all.

So we did. Whilst Wagner's Valkyries rode through the night air, a portion of Murf's ashes went up into the darkness – I picture him and his dog striding forever across the sky.

People ate and drank and laughed and cried and talked about my son and talked about other things. People came long distances for the occasion – from Glasgow, Birmingham, Bristol, Southampton. People met old friends and people they'd never seen before. All the different aspects of my son's life were represented. The fireworks were heard and seen in the next valley. My son's friends from the historical re-enactment group he'd joined at one point gave a gun salute, using a charge made with teaspoonfuls of his ashes. The Going Away Party happened in a space where Murf had enjoyed many legendary parties. This was his last one. And I'm glad it happened, and I'm more grateful than I can ever express to all the people who made it happen and all the people who participated on the night. My son would have loved it, not least the evil smoking sauce, made with chillies that were off the Scoville scale. It was a memorable and fitting tribute to my son. It's good to revisit it in my mind and heart now.

And maybe I need to do something similar for the dragons? This isn't something I can do alone. It will take careful thought and planning, and I will have to enlist help. There are practical issues to resolve too – for example, we will need to figure out a way to get everything we need to the Dragon Field, keep the food hot, make sure we have enough plates and glasses, tables and chairs…

And, of course, I don't know exactly where the Dragon Field is. Up to now I have just found myself there, without any sense of a journey, but I will need a postcode for everyone's satnav… I feel like Alice's White Rabbit. There's so much to do…

But we get there in the end. The weather is kind to us – a gentle breeze blows through the darkness of the October evening, but it's warm enough to be comfortable outdoors and it doesn't rain. Lanterns strung from the trees and flaming torches stuck in the ground provide enough illumination. The Dragon Field, which seemed enormous when I stood here alone, seems almost too small to fit us all in. Everyone is mingling and chatting and there is plenty to eat and drink. The people who helped me before have helped me again. We've even got fireworks! I see through the crowd my friend who brought us rice pudding in the days after my son's death. She's carrying huge quantities of rice pudding now – I hope I manage to get some before it's all gone.

It may seem odd that although I associate rice pudding with my son's death, I find I've developed a serious rice-pudding habit now. What I really associate it with is the sense of people closing ranks round us, offering support and love in those first difficult days. I'm glad she's brought some tonight. Nobody could fix what had happened to my son. He was irrevocably and irretrievably dead, and remains relentlessly dead whatever I do. So people did what was possible and sent flowers or rice pudding or a good bottle of whisky and sat with us and talked about him in his life, kept his memory vivid. So rice pudding has become the unlikely symbol of all of that care and concern and human feeling that upheld me then and continues to uphold me now. I hope the Dragons like rice pudding.

I look round the field, looking for the dragons in the crowd. I'm pleased to see that Oliver – remember him? – is here with a glass of something interesting in his hand. I see Dr R, too, the consultant who was kind to me, making his way to the food table. I realise that I am here in all my avatars – there's me in the spacesuit, alive again, me in the fur-lined arctic parka, me in armour… I really hope that there's no version of me dirty, half naked and covered in leeches – oops! There I am, leeches and all, but maybe nobody will notice. I see with a smile that my friends the mandrills have come down from the trees and are mingling easily with the other guests. And there I am in my clown suit, with all the other clowns, seeking the Laphroaig. Maybe we can do our act later? My Dark Side is here, too, I see, hiding away in the shadows. I wave to her to come and join me and she slides over. I haven't found the dragons yet, but I see my family circulating through the crowd, making sure everyone has enough to eat and drink. I hope that everyone is having fun.

I see other versions of me, too, at all the points of splitting, all the points in my life where a part of me was left behind.

There's me, aged seven, in a hospital bed, talking to a tree. Me in another hospital bed, waiting for the nurse to wheel me to the neonatal intensive care unit where my premature and very sick baby fights for his life. Me on a dark, rainy evening, walking back to my car with my mum and sisters after my father's life support has been switched off in the hospital A&E department. Me sitting in my chair in the conservatory, book in hand. It's 9.16 p.m. on Monday, 16 May 2016. My phone rings, and I wonder for a moment why my son's friend is ringing me. I know even before he speaks. And me again, on another dark, rainy evening in another hospital, with my husband's mobile phone in my hand… All of me is here in this small space. And the world continues to turn and change.

But as I scan round the field, I see that the Dragons haven't arrived yet, which is a bit of a worry. I have warned everyone that we will have some unusual guests, but given reassurance that they are friends, even though they may look a little fierce…

So where are they?

As I walk through the crowd of people, I see the dragons beginning to appear, once again in a circle, all around the perimeter of the field. There must be more of them this time because they form a much bigger circle than before. They are much more solid and visible than they were during our previous encounters, and I see them quite clearly now. Some of them I recognise at last – they are my son's dragons come to life, all colours, shapes and sizes. A Labrador-sized bronze-coloured dragon seems to be in charge, and I recognise her as the dragon we bought in the Rynek Główny, or Grand Square, in Kraków on a trip to Poland many years ago. She bows a gracious acceptance as my friend hands over the rice pudding. I see some of the other dragons have bowls of curry, or glasses of Anarchy Ale in their... hands? Claws? Hands, I think. Others seem to be chatting to some of the guests, who seem quite unfazed by the dragonish presence. There's Dr R talking to the beautiful sea dragon, and my son's re-enactor friends in a huddle with the huge dragon who carries a sword. DEATH, on his white horse, hovers nearby inevitably and always. I need to thread my way through the crowd, get closer, talk to the dragons... I've got it right this time.

Except I haven't. As I get closer to the dragons, I see them, yet again, look at me and begin to shake their heads, as they quite slowly and deliberately dematerialise and fade from view. The rice pudding disappears with them. Next day, as I clear the litter from the field, I find a note, written in purple ink on a ragged piece of parchment. I squint at the elaborate, old-fashioned script until I can decipher what it says. '*Thanks for the rice pudding. Tell your friend we enjoyed it. We will see you later xxx.*'

Time for me to think again. It was a good party, though.

– 33 –

CONVERSATIONS WITH LOVELY DONALD

I've written, rewritten and re-rewritten this chapter several times now. I find I can't reproduce some of these conversations – my hands refuse to write them, my memory shies away from them and my brain reverberates in disbelief that they ever happened. Did they? Have I imagined them? Dreamt them? They felt chilling, unreal, impossible in the context of the Lovely Donald I'd known for over half my life.

Once I'd read that Lollipop text message and absorbed its meaning and implications, I had, I suppose, some unthought-about assumptions about how Lovely Donald would react when I confronted him. I assumed that he had somehow allowed himself to get involved with a woman he'd met, perhaps on a counselling course. I assumed he'd feel some guilt, some sense of wrongdoing, an awareness that he'd betrayed not only me but all the values he professed to hold. I assumed he would apologise, feel some regret about causing me pain and humiliation. As the text message made the nature of the relationship too clear to be deniable, I assumed he would tell me the truth about what had happened.

Over the next four months, every single one of my assumptions was proved wrong.

There's always more than one way to tell a story, more than one standpoint from which events can be viewed. And what you see, after all, depends upon where you are standing. No one else was present during these conversations, so I have only my memory to rely on, and a part of me would want to believe that I somehow misunderstood or misheard what Lovely Donald said. That's a comfort denied to me, though. There were many conversations over many weeks. I asked the same questions in many different ways, but I never found what I was looking for.

The day after I'd returned Lovely Donald's phone to him, I went back to the High Dependency Unit at visiting time. Lovely Donald took my hand, thanked me for coming back, expressed surprise and gratitude. He'd thought, he said, that he'd never see me again, that I'd sever all contact with him and change the locks on my doors. Having lived with me for thirty-four years, he should have known that at the very least I would want some kind of explanation. He should have known, too, that given my own professional background and beliefs, I wouldn't just dump him on the hospital or on my stepson in that way. Whatever the rights and wrongs of the situation, half of our house was his. We had bills to pay, dogs to look after, pensions to discuss…

Lovely Donald thought we could start from now, stay

together, try to rebuild a relationship. I pointed out that he'd always known full well that the worst thing he could do to me was deceive me – far worse, for me, than the sexual betrayal. And he'd deceived me in the cruellest possible ways over years. Any more lies, I said, and I'm gone. And, as I'm sure you'll recall, I wanted to start with a full and frank disclosure of all that had happened.

Of course, said Lovely Donald, he understood totally. He proceeded to tell me how he'd felt entitled to a bit of excitement as he'd grown older – so when he found himself, all accidentally, on a dating website one day, he couldn't resist browsing through the profiles of the women there. He hadn't put up a profile himself, he said, he'd just browsed through what was on offer. He didn't think it was funny when I said that he made it sound like looking through an Argos catalogue.

Linda was the first and only person he'd approached, he said. He'd liked the look of her photograph and thought she'd be up for a bit of extramarital no-strings sex – that's why she was there, after all. Their relationship lasted just short of two years, he said, and ended in 2009 when his prostate problems worsened. Then – how strange! – all of a sudden and quite out of the blue, Linda had sent him that 'Lollipop' text after five years of no contact. He didn't know why she'd sent it, but he'd replied, and they'd had some contact by phone for a while until it just fizzled out. The message after our son died? Oh, he'd just sent a 'howl of pain' to everyone in his address book, and Linda, among others, had replied. Do you believe a word of this? Do dating sites even work like this? I didn't find any of it even remotely credible, and said so. This was Lovely Donald's story, though, and he stuck to it, aided by Friend Dick, until I found the emails some six weeks later.

Lovely Donald then had no choice but to admit that his relationship with Linda had lasted longer than two years – but said he hadn't lied because they'd only had an affair for two years. For the rest of the time, despite all the 'I love you' emails, the relationship had been platonic, a 'loving friendship' – how I grew to hate that phrase. It didn't count. All the sexual references in the emails were fantasy, Lovely Donald 'reliving past glories'. He really did say that, I promise. As if it were the most natural and reasonable thing in the world. I was back in the Hall of Mirrors, everything distorted and unreal.

I could detail other conversations, when Lovely Donald said he felt no guilt, either as we spoke or at the time he was seeing Linda. He did not see why he should feel guilt since he was entitled to have a bit of fun and excitement. It was fun, too, to know that he could fool everyone, that nobody suspected he had a double life. He talked about making opportunities to visit massage parlours or nip over to Yorkshire for a quick fuck or a burger and conversation in the car up on Ilkley Moor if a fuck wasn't on offer. He'd say he was going to a football match, or working. He might even *be* working, but if he was having a quiet shift in his paid job as a night-duty social worker, he'd steal a few hours to drive over to see Linda. There was nothing wrong with this, he said. It was only a ninety-mile round trip. He always had his mobile phone with him. Even at the height of passion, he could answer the phone, put his trousers back on and get to work if a job came up. People would just have to wait – they'd have to wait, after all, if he'd been busy with another job, so what's the difference? I could only shake my head in… what? Despair? Horror? Disbelief? Incomprehension? Something like that. All of that. Sadness.

I'm getting a headache just giving you this expurgated version of my conversations with Lovely Donald. I think I kept on talking to him because I could hardly catch up with this new version of Donald and the disappearance of Donald as I thought I knew him. I think I kept expecting that the real Donald would suddenly reappear, and that somehow all this was a joke or a nightmare. I suppose that's what buffering is like.

You might not believe me if I gave you the unexpurgated version of my conversations with Lovely Donald, even if I could dredge the detail from wherever it has buried itself in my memory. Some of them were so chilling, so unpleasant that I don't think I want to relive or remember them. Donald was never threatening or aggressive and rarely angry. It was his complete unconcern about the impact of his actions on me, on his children and on people who trusted him, and his complete inability to see that he'd done anything wrong that I found chilling. He understood that other people might think he'd done something wrong, so didn't want me to tell anyone else what I learned – but his concern was only about how he would be regarded by others, his image as a good man being lost. As long as no one knew, there wasn't any problem. He'd been faithful for the last three years, after all, and this had been the best time of his life. What about our son? I asked. Silence.

I've had enough now. As time went by and I read the emails, learned that Donald had not deleted Linda's contact details from his phone but had hidden them under his sister's name, as I picked up the odd comment accidentally, perhaps, let slip by Friend Dick and, eventually, had some communication with Lollipop Linda herself, it became obvious and undeniable that everything Lovely Donald had said to me was a lie – or, at best, a half-truth. It saddens me that the final conversation I had with him before he died was all lies.

Perhaps, like his good friend Dick, Lovely Donald believed that I did not know my own best interests. I might think I wanted to know the truth, but they knew better than I did what was good for me. Perhaps he could no longer distinguish truth from lies. Perhaps he just panicked. Or something else altogether. We can't know, can we?

You've probably noticed by now that I tend to repeat myself, and I've probably already told you some of this before. I think I have a kind of obscure feeling that if I tell the story again, maybe in slightly different words, or focusing on slightly different details, perhaps it will begin to make sense. But it doesn't.

Lovely Donald did tell some truths, though. He said over and over again that he had a Dark Side. He certainly did. He also said that he was crap at close personal relationships, and you'll hear no argument from me about that.

If you can make any sense out of all of this, do, please, come and talk to me, explain it to me. I would like nothing better than to understand. I doubt I'll be hearing from you any time soon, though. And I hear you asking me if I've forgiven them, these people who stole my life and my memories – Lovely Donald, Lollipop Linda and Friend Dick. What do you think? *Forgiveness* is one of those words that can have many meanings, and I haven't forgiven them in the sense of condoning their behaviour. They used deceit as a tool to allow them to exercise power in my life and my son's life over many years, without our knowledge and without our consent. Abstract concepts such as loyalty, commitment and honesty – all the qualities Lovely Donald preached about in his sermons – seemed to matter nothing when set against satisfying their own wants. Lovely Donald also, as I learned after his death, misused the power he had in the lives of his sons by his first wife. Even if I can forgive his lack of care for me, I don't forgive his lack of care for his children, all of them. I don't forgive the hypocrisy.

However, Lovely Donald et al had power enough for long enough, and I don't choose to allow them to have power in my life now. I hope that both my stepsons, once they get over all the revelations of their father's final months, can get on with their lives unfettered by the past. Even were we able to get answers from Donald, Linda or Dick, how could we rely on the truthfulness of anything they said? These things have happened and can't be changed. So we have to absorb them into our experience and move on.

Not many people know this story, but I have been distressed by the percentage of those who do who have said to me that Lovely Donald's behaviour proves that all clergy are hypocrites. It doesn't, you know – you can't draw conclusions about categories of people from the behaviour of one individual.

Some clergy are hypocrites; the majority are good, sincere people trying to do an honest job.

Donald, Linda and Dick can only have power in my life now if I give it to them by keeping them in my thoughts and allowing myself to continue to be damaged by dwelling on hatred, resentment or anger. Those wolves have to go hungry, I'm afraid, and – sorry for the mixed metaphor – I have other fish to fry now and a life to lead. I have to grieve for the past, and take a step towards the future.

Perhaps the most telling conversation with Lovely Donald was one he had not with me but with his son, my elder stepson, soon after Murf died.

Lovely Donald: I've fucked up everything all my life.

C (stepson): What do you mean?

Lovely Donald: Silence…

— 34 —

HOODWINKED HATTIE

That's me, I guess. I might not like to think that I was hoodwinked, but I have to accept that I was, whether I like it or not. I have the occasional shivery thought that because I trusted Lovely Donald, that might have led other people to suppress any doubts or questions in their own minds because they trusted me. I don't dwell on those thoughts, but I can't prevent them from shoving their way into my mind sometimes, using their sharp elbows to find a space for themselves.

As I've reflected on being Hoodwinked Hattie, it's occurred to me that it's possible to tell this story in a much simpler, more binary form – a tale of goodies and baddies. Lovely Donald can be seen as the villain, with the rest of us, one way or another, being his victims. Or Lollipop Linda might be the villain – a home-wrecking temptress, luring a basically good man into wrongdoing through her sexual allure. Or I might be the villain – a dark, destructive figure, emasculating both husband and son, driving them to death and betrayal, wearing their heads round my waist like the Dark Kali, mother as destroyer. And let's not forget Friend Dick. He too could be the villain, dropping poison into Donald's ear, working out his own hatred of women through Donald's actions.

But it's all a bit messier and more complicated than that, isn't it? What do you think?

For me it seems much more a story of damage – damaged people playing out that damage in dysfunctional ways. Damage perpetuating damage. My son used to tell me that he thought I was naïve. I'd point to the work I've done over the years and asked how could I be naïve after all that? Well, he'd say, I chose to surround myself with what he would call 'decent' people, and this, in his view, gave me a distorted view of humanity as a whole. I somehow never joined the dots, never saw until it was too late the pattern made by Lovely Donald's behaviour over the years. One of my nieces made what felt like an acute observation recently. My professional training and experience, she said, gave me an understanding of attachment theory and the potential impact of adoption. Other women, without that knowledge, might have been quicker on the uptake, less easy to deceive, because they might have been less likely to make allowances and more likely to trust their intuitions. Is she right?

Just as I see my son as having been damaged by the trauma of his first weeks of life, his necessary isolation from human contact, so too I wonder about Lovely Donald's earliest experiences, *abandoned*, as it must have felt to him, in a nursery at the age of six weeks and left there until he was ten months old. Did that leave him with some complex and destructive issues around women, mothers, wives? Some changes to the hardwiring of his brain? Who knows? It's easy to judge people, but maybe it might be more helpful to try to understand, I reflect. As I walked my dogs round the lake in the pouring rain this morning, it occurred to me that maybe Donald did tell the truth about himself sometimes. Maybe, given his personality, upbringing and experience, he **was** doing the best he could do as a husband and father, even though his best was poor. His truth, after all, was different from mine, and maybe in his truth I was someone to be reacted against, punished in some way. All these thoughts and speculations revolve endlessly in my mind but need to be released eventually. Eventually the gale must die down and the windmill sails come to stillness.

We can't understand what cannot be understood. I can never resolve the contradictions between Donald's actions and behaviours in areas of his professional life, where he seems to have functioned well, and his actions and behaviours with regard to his family. As John Lennon might say, let it be.

I might seem to you to be cold-blooded because I am not denouncing Lovely Donald; nor am I huddled in a tear-soaked heap somewhere. That's not my way. There are a couple of things I've learned in my life about myself – and it could well be that as my son also used to say, I'm weird. I will not be upset if you agree with him. Just as we deal with grief in our own individual ways, so too do we deal with pain.

I was seriously ill and in hospital when I was seven, and was, for a time, in considerable pain. I'd also become completely deaf, so that nobody could explain to me what was happening until a clever doctor hit on the idea of writing basic information down for me – luckily I was a precocious reader. What I learned then, and what has stayed with me ever since, was that thrashing about and fighting made the pain worse, and meant it took the doctors and nurses longer to do what they had to do. The best thing for me, I realised, was to be still, to remember to breathe, and to let the medics do their job as quickly as possible. It helped, I quickly understood, if I could widen my awareness out beyond the pain to include other things in my immediate environment. So I spent a lot of time watching the birds in the tree outside my window, telling myself ever more fantastic stories about their adventures. (There weren't really any vultures in Manchester in 1958, at least not avian ones.) The pain was still there, of course, still painful – but now it had to compete for my attention with the superhero birds. Making this conscious choice to widen out my awareness, while not denying the pain, has helped me over the last sixty years to bear other pain, both physical and emotional. It's helping me now.

Maybe, too, an inevitable result of being the oldest child in a large family has been that I've always known that when I am suffering, other people around me are probably suffering too. We can suffer together and support each other, and that helps me more than collapse or drama, making myself the centre of whatever is going on, and thus adding to the suffering of everyone around me. Even when my son died – the worst thing that has happened in my fairly long life – it helped me to maintain the small routines of daily life, keep some kind of structure, take each day as it came. I couldn't think too far ahead, but I knew that there were some things I needed to do, that I would regret not doing. My son was in the mortuary for six weeks, and I did not want him to be alone all that time. Being dead was a new experience for him, after all. So I held myself together, visited him as often as I could, spent time with him, got to know the staff who were looking after him. Sometimes his former girlfriend came with me, and I was grateful for her company. She tidied his hair and painted his nails, in good Goth fashion, so that he would be ready for his funeral. Lovely Donald chose not to join me for most of those visits, and that was fine. As I've said, each of us grieves in our own way.

And that's important. Please don't judge how I or anyone deals with grief and pain just because it might differ from your own preferred coping strategies. There is no template for these things, no right way. And Lovely Donald and I were, I still believe, united in this. Once again, I can see us, still with a gin and tonic in our hands, singing, 'I did it my-y-y-y-y-y-y-y-y-y way!' We had to. There was no avoiding a collision with this pain, this grief.

When faced with pain that is too big for struggle, once I have done everything that can be done on a practical level to fix things, I find my best plan is to sit with the pain, wait for it to recede. Here's what I tell myself. 'This too shall pass.' I know that my grief for my son will never pass, will remain with me until my final breath, but I know, too, that it will change. It will not grow smaller, but it will become more familiar, more bearable, and I will begin, sooner or later, to allow myself to see life continuing around the edges of the grief.

Call me a control freak – you could be right – but something else that Lovely Donald and I were united on was that the last thing we could do for our son was to stand up, be proud of him, and celebrate his life in all its fullness and complexity, not allow him to be defined solely by the manner of his death. We wanted to make his funeral an occasion that reflected who he was, virtues and failings alike, and showed clearly how much he was loved.

So he was carried in his coffin into the church where his funeral was to be held to the strains of *The Ride of the Valkyries*. His pallbearers were his two half-brothers, two pirates and two dramatically dressed Goths. Everyone said that our son would have approved. It was all highly appropriate to who he was, as were the fireworks that came later, at his Going Away Party.

So my first response when my marriage and my life as I knew it were blown up so dramatically by the Lollipop text was not to denounce Lovely Donald or destroy his possessions. My first response was to sit in my kitchen in the dark and absorb the blast from the explosion. Then, odd as it may seem, I went to sleep.

I had to wake up, though. At first I wanted to protect my stepsons, my family and all those who loved and trusted Lovely Donald from the shock I'd experienced. At first, for a time, I believed this might be possible. I've already recounted how I was unable to sustain the pretence required to keep Lovely Donald's secrets, how people close to me became suspicious. But for those six weeks when I was the only person who knew about Lovely Donald's hidden life, apart from those involved in it, I had to keep up appearances – visit Lovely Donald in hospital, deal with enquiries from concerned others, talk to hospital staff, shop for whatever Lovely Donald needed. I thought – wrongly – that any signs of stress or distress that I might betray would be assumed to be due to the traumas of my son's death, and Lovely Donald's difficult behaviour over the previous year, culminating in his admission to hospital. I wanted time to think, to consider. And I did believe, for a time, that an honest dialogue with Lovely Donald might somehow be possible. Call me stupid if you like. I won't argue.

What struck me throughout that time was that I could not comprehend how Lovely Donald had kept up so much pretence for so long in so many situations. Like I said before, my head would have exploded.

It was not difficult, though, for me to show concern for Lovely Donald, despite my anger. I *felt* concern. He was my son's father. We'd planned his conception together and we'd planned his funeral together. We'd shared our lives for thirty-four years. That meant something to me and I did not know, back then, how little it all meant to Lovely Donald. Exhaustion played its part too. I don't think I've ever felt so tired in my life.

And Lovely Donald continued to shuffle and wriggle and evade all my pleas for some honesty, some straight-talking. I became angry – even more draining and tiring – and I felt deeply, deeply insulted – not only by the betrayal but by the fatuousness of some of the lies he told. How could he think for a moment that I'd believe such obvious nonsense? His language of entitlement left me – I'm not sure where. Reeling? Buffering? Off balance? In shock? All of the above?

Once Friend Dick started to wade in with his contributions, I actually began to feel as if I were being physically attacked. I expected to find bruising and was surprised when none was apparent. I might, in some ways, have preferred a physical attack to the emotional onslaught I faced.

All I could do was to pick my way as carefully as I could through each day, look after the dogs, visit Lovely Donald, try to make some sense of it all…

'Do you feel like you've been used?' asked Friend Dick, smiling like a crocodile. The *Urban Dictionary* defines a crocodile smile thus:

A sly or sinister smirk. While a real smile conveys warmth, this smile is given to hide evil intent. Popular with politicians, crooks and phony friends.

And beware! And be aware – that's how it felt to me at the time. I was not at my best. I could have been doing Friend Dick an injustice.

Time passed and has continued to pass. Lovely Donald continued to lie until he died of a surfeit of lies. I saw the text he'd begun to write to Linda a few days before his death. He never finished or sent it. It said: '*Hattie unfortunately found a text…*' I suppose that's one way to put it. And if you are wondering why he hadn't simply deleted all his incriminating texts and emails – pass. I've no idea.

After Donald's death, his sons and I planned his funeral. I tried, for their sake, to give him a good send-off without compromising myself completely. I threatened Friend Dick with dreadful consequences if he insisted on including, in his part of Donald's eulogy, a reference to Donald being a devoted husband and father. He removed that bit, with just a token protest. Now, this week, I am organising Donald's headstone. This is almost the last practical task I will need to do.

And time has passed. I remember conversations with Lovely Donald over the years, about how our marriage could be quite a lonely place for me. I remember his replies, about caring for me and doing his best. And I've probably told you all this before. One of the effects of shock, I've found, is that I repeat myself, rather like the Ancient Mariner in Coleridge's poem, as if in the repetition I might find some explanation. I never do.

It's time to let go of my marriage and all its complexities now. I grieve for my life and for Lovely Donald's dishonesty – which cost him everything. But I grieve, most of all, for my son.

And I am where I am. I will not be defined by Lovely Donald's attitudes and behaviour towards me. I will not be a victim. Yes – I was hoodwinked. But I will not go through the remainder of my life as Hoodwinked Hattie. I am myself, and there are other things about me far more important than the fact that I was deceived. Let's drop the 'Hoodwinked'. Just call me Hattie. It's not my name but I'll answer to it.

When I was in the shower the other day, a realisation came to me. It's funny how often that happens when I'm in the shower, as if the act of cleansing the body somehow clears the mind.

Think for a moment. Even if I were in reality the shrew of Donald's imagination, even if I were the Dark Kali incarnate, how would that justify his actions? Even if it were true that my son disliked me and needed his father's support to cope with me, how would his father fucking a woman in Yorkshire have helped? Lovely Donald did have choices. He could have chosen to try to put some effort and commitment into his marriage, his family, to try to make life better for all of us. If that felt impossible, he could have been honest and suggested we separate, or take the 'get out of jail free' card I offered him when I suggested we consider separation.

Lovely Donald did what he wanted to do because he could, and because he knew that I was trusting enough that it would never occur to me to check his phone or his emails, or check that he was where he said he was going to be. I trusted him and he knew that and he made a choice to abuse my trust. His choice. His responsibility.

In trying to make sense of it all, I've been doing, I realise, what women do – taking the blame. I've asked myself what I did to contribute to what happened. Was I a bad wife? A bad mother? Did I somehow drive Lovely Donald on to dating websites? Was this a co-dependent relationship in some way, with me enabling Donald to play out his addictions?

I've gone round in circles until I eventually lit upon a spiral that at least offers a way out of all that circular thinking. I was in no way responsible for Donald's choices and actions any more than he was responsible for mine. I'm sure I was never the world's greatest wife or mother – but I don't think I was any worse than the average woman, after all. I did try. I encouraged Donald to work with me to try to improve things. He always refused, just as he refused, all his life, to look at himself and examine how he functioned in family life, the damage he caused.

I've paid for the mistake I made in not knowing when to give up. Lovely Donald paid, at the end of his life, as all his deceptions and self-justifications were exposed in front of his eyes. Despite everything, I'd rather be me, the deceived, than be the deceiver.

Looking at Lovely Donald now from the outside, he seems to have been able to show care, even empathy, towards people with whom he had a professional relationship and a role to play. As a clergyman or social worker, he had a kind of script. He knew what was expected of him. I'm no longer sure about his role as a therapist in the light of Friend Dick's hastily withdrawn remarks about loving friendships with clients.

In the messier and more amorphous roles of personal relationships and family life, though, Lovely Donald seems to have got lost. He seems to have seen us, and me in particular, less as equal human beings with feelings, wants and needs of our own, and more as adjuncts, screens on which he could project whatever complex and negative images he needed to project. So by his own lights, he wasn't betraying and deceiving real people, but just watching flickering images in a kind of silent movie. And when our son died, and then when I found the Lollipop text, suddenly we became real people for Lovely Donald, and our realness overwhelmed him.

That's my theory, anyway. And it's just a theory –

unverifiable, unprovable and possibly totally wrong. I could be overcomplicating all this, overthinking it. You draw your own conclusions.

Lovely Donald used to refer to himself as an onion, having many layers. Father Andrew pointed out after his death, that as well as being many-layered, onions make you cry. But Lovely Donald's food analogies always made me smile. And I've tried to retain some sense of him as the person described to me by so many people – the good and likeable person who helped them through difficult times. All part of the onion, the contradictions.

I'm sure all the questions I've wrestled with are bound to surface from time to time in my mind, along with the pain, humiliation, anger, self-doubt and sorrow that I've lived in over recent months. But it's time to join the ends of my life and carry on, day by day, step by step. Just Hattie, adjusting to life as a widow, of sorts, and a bereaved mother. Just me.

− 35 −

SITTING WITH DRAGONS

The dragons are calling me to the Dragon Field. I can't hear them, but I know they are calling me. So here I am, in the Dragon Field – and it's different this time. The Dragons arrived here before me, and they are clear, solid and distinct. They have brought wooden chairs with them, which look a lot like the battered old chairs from my kitchen. These chairs are too numerous to be mine, but they have the same weathered and well-used look about them – more shabby than shabby-chic.

All the chairs are full of Dragon, I see – except the one next to the bronze Polish Dragon who took the rice pudding. She beckons me to come and sit beside her. As I settle myself down on the chair, two more Dragons appear in front of me, carrying the most beautiful moss-green woollen blanket. They spread the blanket out, and then nestle it round my shoulders to keep me warm and safe. Then two more Dragons come forward, each carrying a cushion. The red Welsh Dragon places her cushion beneath my feet – they've noticed my little short legs! My friend the Sea Dragon carefully places the second cushion on my lap, and motions to me to rest my hands on it, so taking the strain from my shoulders and neck. She makes some adjustment to the blanket, and then all four Dragons return to their seats.

I look around me at the circle of Dragons, and realise that I feel absolutely at home here, in this field, with these Dragons. I feel cared-for, looked-after. I am among friends.

And so we sit. I have a body that is painful much of the time, and so I wriggle about in my chair until I am as comfortable as I can be. I look around me again and see the Dragons, the uncut grasses in the field, buttercups and cornflowers making spots of yellow and blue in the greenness. I can see the trees around the field, now in full leaf, and beyond them, the hills in the distance.

I hear the breeze moving through the grasses and the leaves, and I can hear birdsong all around me. The thought comes that I wish I could identify each bird from its song, as an old woman I used to know was able to do. I notice the thought, but choose not to follow it, bringing my attention back to my body, here on this chair, right now, in this moment.

I see that the bronze Dragon has placed one hand over her heart, and that all the other Dragons are doing the same, one by one. I take my own hand from under the blanket and place it so that I can feel my heart, still beating despite everything. I feel alive.

I close my eyes and follow the movement of my breath, feeling my body swelling as I breathe in, and subsiding with my out-breath.

Behind the thoughts and images that rise up in my mind, as thoughts and images do rise up, I can feel the surge and swell of emotion within me.

Behind my closed eyes, I pay attention to what it is that I am feeling. Flickers of anger crackle and burn as Donald, Linda and Dick come into my mind, and with the anger – bafflement, incomprehension, questioning. How could they do this to me? To anyone? To our family? Feelings of betrayal, rejection, even hatred, surge up, and then self-doubt and a sense of inadequacy twist and swirl through my awareness... jumbled and incoherent thoughts...

I breathe... reconnect with my body on the chair, my breath, and with the emotions within me, which have solidified into a huge sorrow, almost too great for me to bear. I am engulfed in a grey, damp heaviness, pressing me down into nothingness...

I sense movement around me, stretch both hands out to either side of me and grasp the Dragon hands that are reaching out to me in solidarity and support. Hand in hand with Dragons, now, I sit, all of us feeling what we feel. Their feelings are theirs, though. I breathe and settle more deeply into myself.

And there is Grief, waiting for me, as always. Grief for myself and my sufferings. Grief, too, I find, for Donald, Linda and Dick, who all have their own sufferings. Grief, heavy and lumpish in my chest. Images of Donald over the years of our marriage rise up in my awareness, and there is such sadness in my heart that for a moment I find it difficult to breathe at all...

And I can feel my bottom on the chair, my feet on the cushion, so kindly placed by the Red Dragon. I feel the breath rising and falling in my chest and abdomen. And right here, right now, I feel the pressure of the Dragons' hands in mine...

And Grief. I finally follow my son in my mind's eye through the misery and determination of his final hours on this earth as he tried, failed, and tried again to end his life. And succeeded. My son, my son, would I had died for you...

And my body is all Grief now, every cell of my body grieving. I feel my face wet, my hands shaking, even within the Dragons' grasp... And I hear the sound of weeping all around me, as the Dragons grieve for their own suffering, the suffering of those they love and the suffering of those who have injured or betrayed them. I feel the tears that have risen in my own eyes, hot and painful, rolling endlessly down my face... We sit and weep for the pain and sorrow within us.

We grasp hands more tightly, connected in our grieving, but connected, too, in our own strength and in each other's. We can feel what we feel, allow the feelings to be what they are, while we sit here together.

We grieve for ourselves and for each other, for those we love and for those who have harmed us. We grieve, too, for those we have harmed... and we grieve for suffering humanity, the pain of human existence. We grieve for all life on this suffering planet, for the damage inflicted by humankind. For a time there is only grief and tears... and I grieve for the small deaths I witnessed, the mouse gripped in the owl's claws, the buffalo, slaughtered by the Komodo dragon. Let their individual suffering stand for the whole... From Grief grows compassion for all suffering if we allow compassion to grow.

With the Dragons, I surrender myself in this moment to the tidal wave of grief that almost overwhelms me, carries me far out into an ocean of sorrow. But I know that this intensity of feeling will recede eventually. I can experience the emotion, be overwhelmed, but survive and carry on. As the tides recede on the pull of the moon, so the grief will recede as we sit here together. Like the tides, Grief will return in full measure, ebbing and flowing as life continues.

I can weep now, and within the weeping draw on the Dragon strengths around me – the strength of compassion, the support of family and friends, the contact with my son's friends, who loved him too, the companionship of my dogs and the natural world. Everywhere there is beauty if I look for it – in the day-to-day world of the cygnets, in the green spaces and the big skies. There are the small pleasures of daily life to be appreciated – books, good coffee, warm blankets, hot buttered toast, creamy rice pudding…

I move in my chair, hear the sounds around me – and I think the singing bird may be a blackbird. I feel the breath in my body. I open my eyes.

And the Dragons have disappeared, taking with them all the chairs except the four that are from my kitchen, I realise. They've left me the blanket and the cushions, each with a dragon emblem on it. I see they've left a huge box of tissues, open and ready for use. I mop my face, dry my eyes and notice that the front of my T-shirt is wet with tears. Never mind. It will dry. I hear my son's voice very clearly. He is saying, as he would, *We are where we are*. So that's where I have to be.

I see that the ever-thoughtful Dragons have left, on top of a nearby rock, my Mr Happy mug, full of hot camomile tea, together with a plate of toast and a bowl of rice pudding. They've even remembered to leave a proper metal spoon – no plastic cutlery for us. And – kind Dragons – they've brought my little dogs to keep me company. Here they are, sitting patiently by the rock, waiting with every expectation that I will share my toast with them. And I do.

Time to go home.

– 36 –

CODA: AND I ONLY AM ESCAPED ALONE TO TELL THEE...

'Spotting' is a technical term in dance. It's a technique that dancers use while spinning in circles to help them to know how to get back to where they started from without becoming dizzy or losing focus on their posture.

I can never get back to where I started from, when I was a wife and a mother. I can never again see Donald as an honest man. I can never again see my marriage as anything other than a sham. My son's life is over as surely as if he had never existed. I continue to talk to him, but there will never be a reply. When I think about the last thirty-four years of my life, they have an unreal, dream-like quality – but without the sharp, clear images that often come in dreams (mine, at least).

Everything looks blurry, indistinct, as if seen through smoke. I feel moved to make a list:

Things I Can Never Have Again:
* the knowledge that my son is out somewhere in the world, living his life
* the belief that my husband is/was a man of integrity
* the belief that our marriage, whilst not the marriage I might have chosen, did at least have some grounding in affection and shared values
* trust in my own judgement.

Fire, burning hard and fiercely, has ravaged and plundered the landscape of my life. The common moorland grasses and the rare plants have been destroyed. The nests and chicks of the ground-nesting birds are ash. The animals who inhabit this landscape have fled or died. Arsonists have done their worst here, through carelessness or through deliberate actions.

All that remains is the harsh, choking smell of burning and a blackened, burned land.

Lovely Donald's ashes were given the disposal he requested, with one exception. Half were interred in the churchyard of the church where he served as priest for sixteen years; the other half will be scattered illegally at the top of Glastonbury Tor. I could not bring myself, though, to inter his ashes with those of our son, as Lovely Donald had wanted. I just couldn't do it. I didn't want to do it and I'm pretty sure that my son would have felt the same – but I could be wrong. Anyway, it's too late now. There's a part of me that wanted to place my son's ashes with those of the man who was, whatever else, his father – but my body and my instincts rebelled, and this time I listened.

My son's ashes lay in their warm, grey felt casket, and waited for me, indecisive as ever, to choose what should be done with them. All that he was, my baby, my boy, reduced to this heavy pile of ash. '*Fear no more the heat o' the sun,*' my child. You have completed this lifetime, and moved to the next level.

Eventually, almost three years after his death, we held a ceremony to inter Murf's casket of ash in the churchyard of his father's church. I did not put him with his father, but close by.

Of the three of us, I alone remain – not ashes yet, however grey and arid I may feel at times.

And I do have some choice now. I can choose how to live for whatever time remains to me. I can lose myself in anger or grief – or not. I choose not. Our mind creates our reality, and the best thing I can do for my son now, as well as for myself, is to live with some meaning and purpose. To live as well as I can. Not waste the hours and days that are left in impotent misery, resentment or a futile attempt to understand what cannot be understood. I need to pay attention myself to what I tried to tell my son – the point of life is life.

It is only in the last century or so that the death of a child has come to seem an abnormal experience, something wrong in nature. Through most of human history, the majority of people could expect to experience the death of one or more of their children. I do not believe that the ubiquity of the experience made the grief and sense of loss any the less for those bereaved parents than it is for me now. Back to the Bible again:

'*And the King was much moved and went up to the chamber over the gate, and wept: and as he went, thus he said, O my son,*

Absalom, my son, my son Absalom! Would I had died for thee, O Absalom, my son, my son.' (2 Samuel: 18:33)

My son, my son, would I had died for thee. But we don't get to choose. And I need to stop for a few minutes, go for a walk round the house, compose myself.

It's twenty-three minutes later, and I'm back. I've been thinking that perhaps the death of the child who is your only child adds an extra agony to the sense of loss I share with King David. I'm not sure. I do know that the death of your child by his own hand brings almost unbearable pain – why couldn't I save him? Suicide can still, even today, carry a stigma, seem like something that should be hidden. Sod that. My son chose his death and that choice was a part of who he was. I refuse to hide from that or accept any sense of shame. Lovely Donald and I were united, at least, in wanting our son's funeral and later memorial party to express who he was, the fullness of him. We celebrated his life, mourned his death and hid nothing.

Grief and I are accustomed to each other now. We can live with each other, since there is no escape for either of us. My son made his own choices for his own reasons, and while I may feel that he was tragically mistaken, those reasons seemed good to him. I have to accept that because I can't change it. I will carry the weight of it until I take my final breath. That's how it is.

As for Lovely Donald, well, I am not the first – or last – person to experience such a profound rejection and betrayal, to be the 'dupe in Slavic times'. Did you spot the answer to the crossword clue? Of course, it's 'victim'. And I am only a victim if I define myself as such. The details of any betrayal may differ: the central experience remains constant. These things happen; they are part of life. I wish they hadn't been a part of my life – but, once again, I don't get to choose. Rejection and betrayal can't always be avoided or evaded. They happen to somebody; why shouldn't it be me? So all of this is a part of my life, to be lived, experienced and processed. '*What we dwell on, we become*,' and I am not a victim.

If you are wondering what happened to Linda, she is, as I told you, now in a relationship with a widower, in which, she tells me, she feels valued for herself for the first time in her life. No longer Lollipop Linda – let's call her Lucky Linda. Her widower apparently knows all about her relationship with Lovely Donald, and was seemingly unperturbed that she remained in some kind of contact with him until about ten days before his death. Lucky Linda, too, surrounded by her children and grandchildren – though she has not escaped grief and loss in her family. My Dark Side mutters, *It's not fair*, but I don't listen. Life is not fair. What has fairness to do with any of it? My Dark Side retreats, a bit shamefacedly.

As for Friend Dick, he remains an enigma. I have no more to say of him.

So here I am and here I stand, the dragons at my back. Having chosen to put my Sabatier knives back in their knife block, here I must remain for now. I have paid my membership dues to *Dignitas* as against the day, which may never come, when my illness progresses to the point of unbearability. I like to be prepared. Grief remains my constant and unchanging companion, but I see life blossom in the spaces around the grief. I remember every day that the point of life is life.

I am an atom in the stream of life, one more small point of light in the darkness and mystery of existence. No more and no less important than all the other small points of light in this Milky Way. We are, all of us, part of an interconnected wholeness.

'*And I only am escaped alone to tell thee.*' (Job 1:15) So I must make the best fist I can of what remains.

The End

ACKNOWLEDGEMENTS

It is now five years since my son's death, and three years since the death of Lovely Donald. If I were to list individually all the people who have offered me help, support and love over the last five years, I'd have to write another book. I've come to think of all these people as 'The Helpers', to whom this book is dedicated. Through them I've learned the real value of kindness. Without them I doubt I'd still be here. Some of them, like the personal shoppers who chose an outfit for me to wear for my son's funeral, may never know the value of their actions and kindness, but I do. So – thank you to all The Helpers. Once again I meet the inadequacy of words, so it's best to keep it simple. Thank you all.

I'm grateful to my family, friends, acquaintances and strangers for all the help, care and support I've been given through the worst time in my life. I'm thankful, too, for my son's friends, who continue to keep in contact with me. Between us, through our conversations and shared memories, he continues to have a kind of life and he is not forgotten.

Thanks, too, to Nick from Cornerstones, (aka the Dragon Nicmentor), whose professionalism and endless patience (and kindness, of course) helped make this a better book.

Finally, thanks to everyone at SPP for putting up with my endless dithering. All failings and errors in the book are, of course, my own.

Hattie Annie Jones
May 2021